Presented to

_____

By

_____

On the Occasion of

_____

Date

_____

The Bible
Promise Book
for Women

BARBOUR
PUBLISHING

Chapter introductions written by Tina Krause.

ISBN 978-1-61626-358-4
Special Edition ISBN: 978-1-63058-381-1

Scripture quotations marked kjv are taken from the King James Version of the Bible.

Scripture quotations marked niv are taken from the Holy Bible, New International Version®. niv®. Copyright © 1973, 1978, 1984 by International Bible Society. Used by permission of Zondervan. All rights reserved.

Scripture quotations marked nasb are taken from the New American Standard Bible, © 1960, 1962, 1963, 1968, 1971, 1972, 1973, 1975, 1977, 1995 by The Lockman Foundation. Used by permission.

Scripture quotations marked nkjv are taken from the New King James Version®. Copyright © 1982 by Thomas Nelson, Inc. Used by permission. All rights reserved.

Scripture quotations marked nlt are taken from the *Holy Bible*, New Living Translation, copyright © 1996, 2004. Used by permission of Tyndale House Publishers, Inc. Wheaton, Illinois 60189, U.S.A. All rights reserved.

Published by Barbour Publishing, Inc., P.O. Box 719, Uhrichsville, Ohio 44683
www.barbourbooks.com

Our mission is to publish and distribute inspirational products offering exceptional value and biblical encouragement to the masses.

Member of the
Evangelical Christian
Publishers Association

Printed in China.

Contents

Introduction

Our world sends many conflicting signals on the important issues of life. How should we approach anger? Is discipline a good thing or not? Why speak with honesty? Is prayer for real? What is true wisdom?

In His kindness, God has answered all of these questions—and many more—in the pages of His Word, the Bible. Whatever our needs, we can find in scripture the principles we need to address the issues we face.

This collection of Bible verses is a handy reference to some of the key issues that all people—and especially women—face. In these pages, you'll find carefully selected verses that address topics like comfort, encouragement, friendship, purity, rest, and understanding. In fact, more than five dozen categories are covered, arranged alphabetically for ease of use.

This book is not intended to replace regular, personal Bible study. Nor is it a replacement for a good concordance for in-depth study of a particular subject. It is, however, a quick reference to some of the key issues of life that women most often face. We hope it will be an encouragement to you as you read.

Adversity

No one is exempt from problems. From the palace to the poorhouse, women throughout the ages have fought and conquered adversity in their lives.

Queen Esther risked losing her only relative and her people. Using her influence, she saved the Israelites from destruction. Interestingly, the Jewish name *Esther* means "Hadassah," which comes from the word *myrtle*—the tree whose leaves only release fragrance when they are crushed.

Are you facing adversity? Perhaps your faith has brought reproach or daily struggles have robbed your faith. Regardless, the scriptures ease the crush of adversity, releasing the sweet fragrance of God's overcoming power.

For I reckon that the sufferings of this present time are not worthy to be compared with the glory which shall be revealed in us.
ROMANS 8:18 KJV

For just as the sufferings of Christ flow over into our lives, so also through Christ our comfort overflows. If we are distressed, it is for your comfort and salvation; if we are comforted, it is for your comfort, which produces in you patient endurance of the same sufferings we suffer.
2 CORINTHIANS 1:5–6 NIV

If you are reviled for the name of Christ, you are blessed, because the Spirit of glory and of God rests on you.
1 PETER 4:14 NASB

These things I have spoken to you, that in Me you may have peace. In the world you will have tribulation; but be of good cheer, I have overcome the world.
JOHN 16:33 NKJV

That the trial of your faith, being much more precious than of gold that perisheth, though it be tried with fire, might be found unto praise and honour and glory at the appearing of Jesus Christ.
1 PETER 1:7 KJV

I want to know Christ and experience the mighty power that raised him from the dead. I want to suffer with him, sharing in his death, so that one way or another I will experience the resurrection from the dead!
PHILIPPIANS 3:10–11 NLT

After you have suffered for a little while, the God of all grace,
who called you to His eternal glory in Christ, will Himself
perfect, confirm, strengthen and establish you.
1 PETER 5:10 NASB

> Blessed are you when men hate you, and when they
> exclude you, and revile you, and cast out your
> name as evil, for the Son of Man's sake.
> LUKE 6:22 NKJV

Are any of you suffering hardships?
You should pray.
JAMES 5:13 NLT

> Yea, and all that will live godly in
> Christ Jesus shall suffer persecution.
> 2 TIMOTHY 3:12 KJV

Dear friends, do not be surprised at the painful trial you are
suffering, as though something strange were happening to you.
But rejoice that you participate in the sufferings of Christ,
so that you may be overjoyed when his glory is revealed.
1 PETER 4:12–13 NIV

> For momentary, light affliction is producing for us an eternal
> weight of glory far beyond all comparison.
> 2 CORINTHIANS 4:17 NASB

If we suffer, we shall also reign with him.
2 TIMOTHY 2:12 KJV

For this is commendable, if because of conscience toward God one endures grief, suffering wrongfully. For to this you were called, because Christ also suffered for us, leaving us an example, that you should follow His steps: "Who committed no sin, Nor was deceit found in His mouth"; who, when He was reviled, did not revile in return; when He suffered, He did not threaten, but committed Himself to Him who judges righteously.

1 PETER 2:19, 21–23 NKJV

Our Creator never intended that we should shoulder a load of suffering ourselves. That's the whole purpose of spiritual community.

LINDA BARTLETT

Angels

A near miss. Your car swerves to the side of the road avoiding a collision with an oncoming vehicle. How did you avoid disaster?

Fatigue zaps your strength but you still have much to do. You pray and amazingly you breeze through your work as if unseen hands carried you to complete the task. A coincidence? Or did God dispatch angels to assist you?

Angels are real. Unlike the stereotypical images of chubby-cheeked cherubs, these powerful, angelic beings minister to believers. At God's command, they delivered Paul from prison, shut the lions' mouths, provided for Elijah, and brought an amazing message to Mary.

Chubby-cheeked cherubs? Think again.

And God never said to any of the angels, "Sit in the place of honor at my right hand until I humble your enemies, making them a footstool under your feet." Therefore, angels are only servants—spirits sent to care for people who will inherit salvation.
HEBREWS 1:13–14 NLT

And he shall send his angels with a great sound of a trumpet, and they shall gather together his elect from the four winds, from one end of heaven to the other.
MATTHEW 24:31 KJV

The angel of the LORD encamps around those who fear Him, and rescues them.
PSALM 34:7 NASB

For I am persuaded that neither death nor life, nor angels nor principalities nor powers, nor things present nor things to come, nor height nor depth, nor any other created thing, shall be able to separate us from the love of God which is in Christ Jesus our Lord.
ROMANS 8:38–39 NKJV

On life's busy thoroughfares
We meet with angels
unawares. . . .
HELEN STEINER RICE

Anger

$\mathscr{G}$t doesn't matter who was right or wrong. You *feel* wronged and anger simmers on the verge of full boil.

Can we be angry and not sin? To feel anger is one thing, to act on it is another. When we use our anger to justify our wrongful deeds, we sin.

The Bible, however, gives us clear and concise instructions on how to handle anger or angry people. How can we curb anger, irritations, and flare-ups? Apply the calming influence of God's Word to our circumstance. Ah, yes. That's better.

He who is slow to anger has great understanding,
but he who is quick-tempered exalts folly.
PROVERBS 14:29 NASB

> So then, my beloved brethren, let every man be swift to
> hear, slow to speak, slow to wrath; for the wrath of man
> does not produce the righteousness of God.
> JAMES 1:19–20 NKJV

Don't befriend angry people or associate with hot-tempered people,
or you will learn to be like them and endanger your soul.
PROVERBS 22:24–25 NLT

> Be not hasty in thy spirit to be angry:
> for anger resteth in the bosom of fools.
> ECCLESIASTES 7:9 KJV

Better to live in a desert than with a quarrelsome
and ill-tempered wife.
PROVERBS 21:19 NIV

> Fathers, do not exasperate your children,
> so that they will not lose heart.
> COLOSSIANS 3:21 NASB

A soft answer turns away wrath, but a harsh word stirs up anger.
PROVERBS 15:1 NKJV

> Do everything without complaining and arguing.
> PHILIPPIANS 2:14 NLT

But I tell you that anyone who is angry with his brother will be subject to judgment. Again, anyone who says to his brother, "Raca," is answerable to the Sanhedrin. But anyone who says, "You fool!" will be in danger of the fire of hell.
MATTHEW 5:22 NIV

A wrathful man stirreth up strife:
but he that is slow to anger appeaseth strife.
PROVERBS 15:18 KJV

He who is slow to anger is better than the mighty, and he who rules his spirit, than he who captures a city.
PROVERBS 16:32 NASB

Beloved, do not avenge yourselves, but rather give place to wrath; for it is written, "Vengeance is Mine, I will repay," says the Lord.
ROMANS 12:19 NKJV

Better a dry crust eaten in peace than a house filled with feasting—and conflict.
PROVERBS 17:1 NLT

In your anger do not sin:
Do not let the sun go down while you are still angry.
EPHESIANS 4:26 NIV

Being angry or unforgiving makes it impossible to have a gentle and quiet spirit.
DARLENE WILKINSON

Charity

Women are caregivers by nature. Need a hand? We offer two! Yet sometimes our gift of giving wears old under constant demands and daily responsibilities.

God, however, is the supreme example of charity at work. He saw our neediness and sent His Son, Jesus, to save us from our sins. And He keeps on giving.

Having received so much constrains us to give more liberally. God's charity never ceases and neither should ours. Although needs differ—financial, physical, emotional, or spiritual—human benevolence comes from a giving heart. And our charitable giving begins right where we are.

Blessed is he that considereth the poor: the Lord will deliver him in time of trouble. The Lord will preserve him, and keep him alive; and he shall be blessed upon the earth: and thou wilt not deliver him unto the will of his enemies.
Psalm 41:1–2 kjv

> One who is gracious to a poor man lends to the Lord,
> and He will repay him for his good deed.
> Proverbs 19:17 nasb

But when you give a feast, invite the poor, the maimed, the lame, the blind. And you will be blessed, because they cannot repay you; for you shall be repaid at the resurrection of the just.
Luke 14:13–14 nkjv

> He who despises his neighbor sins,
> but blessed is he who is kind to the needy.
> Proverbs 14:21 niv

I have shewed you all things, how that so labouring ye ought to support the weak, and to remember the words of the Lord Jesus, how he said, It is more blessed to give than to receive.
Acts 20:35 kjv

> He has given freely to the poor, His righteousness endures
> forever; His horn will be exalted in honor.
> Psalm 112:9 nasb

I have been young, and now am old; yet I have not seen the righteous forsaken, nor his descendants begging bread. He is ever merciful, and lends; and his descendants are blessed.
Psalm 37:25–26 nkjv

Teach those who are rich in this world not to be proud and not to trust in their money, which is so unreliable. Their trust should be in God, who richly gives us all we need for our enjoyment. Tell them to use their money to do good. They should be rich in good works and generous to those in need, always being ready to share with others. By doing this they will be storing up their treasure as a good foundation for the future so that they may experience true life.
1 Timothy 6:17–19 nlt

Sell that ye have, and give alms; provide yourselves bags which wax not old, a treasure in the heavens that faileth not, where no thief approacheth, neither moth corrupteth. For where your treasure is, there will your heart be also.
Luke 12:33–34 kjv

Above all, keep fervent in your love for one another, because love covers a multitude of sins. Be hospitable to one another without complaint. As each one has received a special gift, employ it in serving one another as good stewards of the manifold grace of God.
1 Peter 4:8–10 nasb

Give, and it will be given to you: good measure, pressed down, shaken together, and running over will be put into your bosom. For with the same measure that you use, it will be measured back to you.
Luke 6:38 nkjv

Charity begins at home.
Proverb

Comfort

A loved one passes away, and friends and family surround you with prayers and comforting words. Illness strikes a blow, but friends support and comfort you. Problems weigh heavy and there seems no way out, but the scriptures speak comfort to your heart.

Moms comfort their sick children with hugs and chicken soup. Similarly, God eases our pain and lightens our load through the comfort of His Word and His Spirit. Jesus called the Holy Spirit "the Comforter." He is the One who teaches, guides, soothes, and stands with us. The Comforter comforts like no one else can.

Blessed be the God and Father of our Lord Jesus Christ, the Father of mercies and God of all comfort, who comforts us in all our tribulation, that we may be able to comfort those who are in any trouble, with the comfort with which we ourselves are comforted by God.
2 CORINTHIANS 1:3–4 NKJV

> Even when I walk through the darkest valley,
> I will not be afraid, for you are close beside me.
> Your rod and your staff protect and comfort me.
> PSALM 23:4 NLT

He will wipe every tear from their eyes. There will be no more death or mourning or crying or pain, for the old order of things has passed away.
REVELATION 21:4 NIV

> He will swallow up death for all time, and the Lord GOD
> will wipe tears away from all faces, and He will remove the
> reproach of His people from all the earth;
> for the LORD has spoken.
> ISAIAH 25:8 NASB

For the Lord himself shall descend from heaven with a shout, with the voice of the archangel, and with the trump of God: and the dead in Christ shall rise first: Then we which are alive and remain shall be caught up together with them in the clouds, to meet the Lord in the air: and so shall we ever be with the Lord. Wherefore comfort one another with these words.
1 THESSALONIANS 4:16–18 KJV

And I will pray the Father, and he shall give you another
Comforter, that he may abide with you for ever.
JOHN 14:16 KJV

But as for me, I would seek God,
and I would place my cause before God.
JOB 5:8 NASB

You shall increase my greatness,
and comfort me on every side.
PSALM 71:21 NKJV

The Spirit of the Lord GOD is upon me; because the LORD hath anointed
me to preach good tidings unto the meek; he hath sent me to
bind up the brokenhearted, to proclaim liberty to the captives,
and the opening of the prison to them that are bound; to
proclaim the acceptable year of the LORD, and the day of
vengeance of our God; to comfort all that mourn.
ISAIAH 61:1–2 KJV

Teach these new disciples to obey all the commands
I have given you. And be sure of this: I am with you always,
even to the end of the age.
MATTHEW 28:20 NLT

Praise be to the God and Father of our Lord Jesus Christ, the Father of
compassion and the God of all comfort, who comforts us in all
our troubles, so that we can comfort those in any trouble with
the comfort we ourselves have received from God. For just as
the sufferings of Christ flow over into our lives, so also through
Christ our comfort overflows.
2 CORINTHIANS 1:3–5 NIV

I will not leave you comfortless: I will come to you.
JOHN 14:18 KJV

Come to Me, all who are weary and heavy-laden,
and I will give you rest.
MATTHEW 11:28 NASB

I remembered your judgments of old,
O LORD, and have comforted myself.
PSALM 119:52 NKJV

I will comfort you there in Jerusalem
as a mother comforts her child.
ISAIAH 66:13 NLT

Finally, brethren, farewell. Become complete. Be of good
comfort, be of one mind, live in peace; and the God of
love and peace will be with you.
2 CORINTHIANS 13:11 NKJV

Come near to God and he will come near to you. Wash your hands,
you sinners, and purify your hearts, you double-minded.
JAMES 4:8 NIV

*All you really need is the One who promised
never to leave or forsake you—the One who
said, "Lo, I am with you always."*
JONI EARECKSON TADA

Conversation

Have you ever blurted out the wrong words at the wrong time? Mortified, you wish you could push REWIND and start again—but unfortunately, the words are irretrievable.

The scriptures tell us to keep watch over our tongue, and for good reason. Words have the power to create strife or peace; to uplift or destroy; to bless or to curse.

The old adage claims "words will never hurt me." That, however, is untrue. Wrong words *do* hurt, but the right words spoken at the right time have the power to heal and comfort. Words count—so count your words!

So also the tongue is a small part of the body, and yet it boasts of great things. See how great a forest is set aflame by such a small fire!
JAMES 3:5 NASB

A word fitly spoken is like apples of gold in settings of silver.
PROVERBS 25:11 NKJV

Don't make rash promises, and don't be hasty in bringing matters before God. After all, God is in heaven, and you are here on earth. So let your words be few.
ECCLESIASTES 5:2 NLT

A gentle answer turns away wrath,
but a harsh word stirs up anger.
PROVERBS 15:1 NIV

The heart of the righteous studieth to answer: but the mouth of the wicked poureth out evil things.
PROVERBS 15:28 KJV

Let your speech always be with grace, as though seasoned with salt, so that you will know how you should respond to each person.
COLOSSIANS 4:6 NASB

A wise man's heart guides his mouth, and his lips promote instruction. Pleasant words are a honeycomb, sweet to the soul and healing to the bones.
PROVERBS 16:23–24 NIV

A talebearer revealeth secrets:
but he that is of a faithful spirit concealeth the matter.
PROVERBS 11:13 KJV

He who walks in integrity walks securely,
but he who perverts his ways will be found out.
PROVERBS 10:9 NASB

Even if I should choose to boast, I would not be a fool,
because I would be speaking the truth. But I refrain,
so no one will think more of me than is warranted
by what I do or say.
2 CORINTHIANS 12:6 NIV

A fool vents all his feelings, but a wise man holds them back.
PROVERBS 29:11 NKJV

But now is the time to get rid of anger, rage,
malicious behavior, slander, and dirty language.
COLOSSIANS 3:8 NLT

Set a watch, O LORD, before my mouth; keep the door of my lips.
PSALM 141:3 KJV

There is one who speaks rashly like the thrusts of a sword,
but the tongue of the wise brings healing.
PROVERBS 12:18 NASB

We all stumble in many ways. If anyone is never at fault in what he says,
he is a perfect man, able to keep his whole body in check.
JAMES 3:2 NIV

A man has joy by the answer of his mouth,
and a word spoken in due season, how good it is!
PROVERBS 15:23 NKJV

A time to tear and a time to mend. A time to be quiet and a time to speak.
ECCLESIASTES 3:7 NLT

*Kind words can be short and easy to speak,
but their echoes are truly endless.*
MOTHER TERESA

Counsel

Were you ever so immersed in a problem that you felt like you were drowning? Have you ever had to make a decision and didn't know what to do? At those times we turn to God—often through godly counsel, perhaps from a pastor or trusted Christian friend.

We all need counsel and direction sometimes. The old saying that "two heads are better than one" is not only noteworthy, it's scriptural!

King Solomon said that to seek godly counsel is wise. Moreover, to grow spiritually we must maintain an open, teachable spirit.

Good advice comes from God-advice. Now that's good counsel.

As every man hath received the gift, even so minister the same one to another, as good stewards of the manifold grace of God.
1 PETER 4:10 KJV

> For a child will be born to us, a son will be given to us; and the government will rest on His shoulders; and His name will be called Wonderful Counselor, Mighty God, Eternal Father, Prince of Peace.
> ISAIAH 9:6 NASB

All your sons will be taught by the LORD, and great will be your children's peace.
ISAIAH 54:13 NIV

> Now no chastening seems to be joyful for the present, but painful; nevertheless, afterward it yields the peaceable fruit of righteousness to those who have been trained by it.
> HEBREWS 12:11 NKJV

Get all the advice and instruction you can, so you will be wise the rest of your life.
PROVERBS 19:20 NLT

> Howbeit when he, the Spirit of truth, is come, he will guide you into all truth: for he shall not speak of himself; but whatsoever he shall hear, that shall he speak: and he will shew you things to come.
> JOHN 16:13 KJV

Where no counsel is, the people fall: but in the multitude of counsellors there is safety.
PROVERBS 11:14 KJV

Without consultation, plans are frustrated,
but with many counselors they succeed.
PROVERBS 15:22 NASB

Because the Lord disciplines those he loves, and he punishes everyone he
accepts as a son. Endure hardship as discipline; God is treating
you as sons. For what son is not disciplined by his father?
HEBREWS 12:6–7 NIV

A wise man will hear and increase learning,
and a man of understanding will attain wise counsel.
PROVERBS 1:5 NKJV

Two are better than one, because they have a good return for their
work: If one falls down, his friend can help him up. But pity
the man who falls and has no one to help him up!
ECCLESIASTES 4:9–10 NIV

The true secret of giving advice is, after
you have honestly given it, to be perfectly
indifferent whether it is taken or not, and
never persist in trying to set people right.
HANNAH WHITALL SMITH

Courage

$\mathcal{F}$ew of us require the kind of courage that Daniel had when he entered the lions' den or that David exercised when he confronted the giant. Nevertheless, courage is needed to conquer our fears, proclaim our faith, and overcome adversity. Oftentimes, we need courage just to get through the day!

The following verses provide instructions and admonitions to build our faith and fortitude. They equip us with the courage we need to conquer our giants in life's den of lions.

Be strong and very courageous. Be careful to obey all the instructions Moses gave you. Do not deviate from them, turning either to the right or to the left. Then you will be successful in everything you do.
JOSHUA 1:7 NLT

> Wait on the LORD: be of good courage, and he shall strengthen thine heart: wait, I say, on the LORD.
> PSALM 27:14 KJV

For God has not given us a spirit of timidity,
but of power and love and discipline.
2 TIMOTHY 1:7 NASB

> So we say with confidence, "The Lord is my helper; I will not be afraid. What can man do to me?"
> HEBREWS 13:6 NIV

Only let your conduct be worthy of the gospel of Christ, so that whether I come and see you or am absent, I may hear of your affairs, that you stand fast in one spirit, with one mind striving together for the faith of the gospel, and not in any way terrified by your adversaries, which is to them a proof of perdition, but to you of salvation, and that from God.
PHILIPPIANS 1:27–28 NKJV

> And now, dear children, remain in fellowship with Christ so that when he returns, you will be full of courage and not shrink back from him in shame.
> 1 JOHN 2:28 NLT

The wicked man flees though no one pursues,
but the righteous are as bold as a lion.
PROVERBS 28:1 NIV

Therefore, brethren, having boldness to enter the Holiest by the blood of Jesus...by a new and living way which He consecrated for us, through the veil, that is, His flesh, and having a High Priest over the house of God, let us draw near with a true heart in full assurance of faith.

HEBREWS 10:19–22 NKJV

So be strong and courageous, all you who put your hope in the LORD!
PSALM 31:24 NLT

In whom we have boldness and access with confidence by the faith of him.
EPHESIANS 3:12 KJV

You have to accept whatever comes and the only important thing is that you meet it with courage, and with the best you have to give.

ELEANOR ROOSEVELT

Diligence

The author of Ecclesiastes wrote: "Whatever your hand finds to do, do it with all your might." Diligence keeps going while frustration gives up. Diligence acts while procrastination rests. Diligence says, "I can do it" while defeat says, "I can't."

To work with diligence is essential to every facet of our spiritual and physical lives. With devoted tenacity we seek God and His will. With steadfast determination, we pray and study His Word.

Wherever we are or whatever we do, God calls us to remain diligent—even when our greatest efforts seem vain or our hard work goes unnoticed.

I will remember my song in the night; I will meditate with my heart, and my spirit ponders.
PSALM 77:6 NASB

But be very careful to keep the commandment and the law that Moses the servant of the LORD gave you: to love the LORD your God, to walk in all his ways, to obey his commands, to hold fast to him and to serve him with all your heart and all your soul.
JOSHUA 22:5 NIV

Keep your heart with all diligence, for out of it spring the issues of life.
PROVERBS 4:23 NKJV

Since you excel in so many ways—in your faith, your gifted speakers, your knowledge, your enthusiasm, and your love from us—I want you to excel also in this gracious act of giving.
2 CORINTHIANS 8:7 NLT

For this very reason, make every effort to add to your faith goodness; and to goodness, knowledge; and to knowledge, self-control; and to self-control, perseverance; and to perseverance, godliness; and to godliness, brotherly kindness; and to brotherly kindness, love. Therefore, my brothers, be all the more eager to make your calling and election sure. For if you do these things, you will never fall.
2 PETER 1:5–7, 10 NIV

The soul of the sluggard craves and gets nothing, but the soul of the diligent is made fat.
PROVERBS 13:4 NASB

He becometh poor that dealeth with a slack hand:
but the hand of the diligent maketh rich.
PROVERBS 10:4 KJV

Behold that which I have seen: it is good and comely for
one to eat and to drink, and to enjoy the good of all his
labour that he taketh under the sun all the days of his life,
which God giveth him: for it is his portion. Every man also to
whom God hath given riches and wealth, and hath given
him power to eat thereof, and to take his portion, and to
rejoice in his labour; this is the gift of God.
ECCLESIASTES 5:18–19 KJV

But as for you, brethren, do not grow weary of doing good.
2 THESSALONIANS 3:13 NASB

If it is encouraging, let him encourage;
if it is contributing to the needs of others, let him give
generously; if it is leadership, let him govern diligently;
if it is showing mercy, let him do it cheerfully.
ROMANS 12:8 NIV

The plans of the diligent lead surely to plenty, but those of everyone who
is hasty, surely to poverty.
PROVERBS 21:5 NKJV

So let's not get tired of doing what is good. At just the right
time we will reap a harvest of blessing if we don't give up.
GALATIANS 6:9 NLT

Wherefore, beloved, seeing that ye look for such things, be diligent that ye
may be found of him in peace, without spot, and blameless.
2 PETER 3:14 KJV

Whatever is commanded by the God of heaven,
let it be done with zeal for the house of the God of heaven,
so that there will not be wrath against
the kingdom of the king and his sons.

EZRA 7:23 NASB

Therefore, my dear brothers, stand firm. Let nothing move you.
Always give yourselves fully to the work of the Lord,
because you know that your labor in the Lord is not in vain.
1 CORINTHIANS 15:58 NIV

Much food is in the fallow ground of the poor,
and for lack of justice there is waste.

PROVERBS 13:23 NKJV

Whatever your hand finds to do, do it with all your might.
ECCLESIASTES 9:10 NASB

When I stand before God at the end of my
life, I would hope that I would not have a
single bit of talent left, and could say,
"I used everything you gave me."

ERMA BOMBECK

Discipline, Family

Discipline in a Christian home consists of more than issuing commands like, "No video games until you finish your homework!" or, "Stop goofing around before someone gets hurt!"

It's easy to shout directives, but administering loving discipline takes work, thought, and persistence. To establish rules and lovingly implement them is to build structure, providing children with a sense of security. Discipline teaches kids the consequences of sin and the importance of submitting to authority.

Just as God disciplines those He loves, we discipline our children out of love. And contrary to popular thinking, a disciplined child is a happy child.

One that ruleth well his own house, having his children in subjection with all gravity; (For if a man know not how to rule his own house, how shall he take care of the church of God?)
1 TIMOTHY 3:4–5 KJV

Do not withhold correction from a child, for if you beat him with a rod, he will not die. You shall beat him with a rod, and deliver his soul from hell.
PROVERBS 23:13–14 NKJV

Those who spare the rod of discipline hate their children. Those who love their children care enough to discipline them.
PROVERBS 13:24 NLT

Foolishness is bound in the heart of a child; but the rod of correction shall drive it far from him.
PROVERBS 22:15 KJV

Now behold, he has a son who has observed all his father's sins which he committed, and observing does not do likewise. He does not eat at the mountain shrines or lift up his eyes to the idols of the house of Israel, or defile his neighbor's wife, or oppress anyone, or retain a pledge, or commit robbery, but he gives his bread to the hungry and covers the naked with clothing, he keeps his hand from the poor, does not take interest or increase, but executes My ordinances, and walks in My statutes; he will not die for his father's iniquity, he will surely live.
EZEKIEL 18:14–17 NASB

Fathers, do not aggravate your children, or they will become discouraged.
COLOSSIANS 3:21 NLT

Even a child is known by his actions,
by whether his conduct is pure and right.
PROVERBS 20:11 NIV

Fathers, do not provoke your children to anger, but bring
them up in the discipline and instruction of the Lord.
EPHESIANS 6:4 NASB

Discipline your son, and he will give you peace;
he will bring delight to your soul.
PROVERBS 29:17 NIV

I can't think of anything parents could
do to children more heartless than
failing to discipline.
JANETTE OKE

Discipline, God's

Ouch! Did you ever feel like God dispensed a spiritual spanking? Just as we discipline our children, our heavenly Father disciplines us. Why? Because an undisciplined life brings bondage while a disciplined life liberates. Yes, discipline frees us.

The Lord has a good reason for everything He does, and everything He does comes from love. So rather than bemoaning the temporary pain, consider discipline's benefits: It teaches, guides, garners appreciation, gives life, establishes our spiritual "daughtership," and yields the peaceable fruit of righteousness within us.

Admit it. Discipline helps way more than it hurts!

O LORD, do not rebuke me in Your anger,
nor chasten me in Your hot displeasure.
PSALM 6:1 NKJV

I correct and discipline everyone I love.
So be diligent and turn from your indifference.
REVELATION 3:19 NLT

Behold, happy is the man whom God correcteth: therefore despise not thou
the chastening of the Almighty: For he maketh sore,
and bindeth up: he woundeth, and his hands make whole.
JOB 5:17–18 KJV

And you have forgotten the exhortation which is addressed
to you as sons, "My son, do not regard lightly the discipline
of the LORD, nor faint when you are reproved by Him; for
those whom the LORD loves He disciplines, and He scourges
every son whom He receives." It is for discipline that you
endure; God deals with you as with sons; for what son is
there whom his father does not discipline? But if you are
without discipline, of which all have become partakers,
then you are illegitimate children and not sons.
HEBREWS 12:5–8 NASB

Know then in your heart that as a man disciplines his son,
so the LORD your God disciplines you.
DEUTERONOMY 8:5 NIV

For if we would judge ourselves, we would not be judged.
But when we are judged, we are chastened by the Lord,
that we may not be condemned with the world.
1 CORINTHIANS 11:31–32 NKJV

The LORD has punished me severely, but he did not let me die.
PSALM 118:18 NLT

For the commandment is a lamp; and the law is light;
and reproofs of instruction are the way of life.
PROVERBS 6:23 KJV

Blessed is the man whom You chasten, O LORD, and whom You teach
out of Your law; that You may grant him relief from the days
of adversity, until a pit is dug for the wicked.
PSALM 94:12–13 NASB

For whom the LORD loves He corrects,
just as a father the son in whom he delights.
PROVERBS 3:12 NKJV

No discipline is enjoyable while it is happening—it's painful! But afterward
there will be a peaceful harvest of right living for those who are
trained in this way.
HEBREWS 12:11 NLT

God has to punish His children
from time to time
and it is the very
demonstration of His love.

ELISABETH ELLIOT

Duty

What is a Christian woman's duty? The scriptures list a few: to revere, serve, and obey God and keep His commandments.

In the 1940s and '50s a married woman's "duty" was clearly defined—to love and respect her husband while caring for her home and children. Today society has changed. God's Word, however, remains the same.

Our duty to love and respect our husbands, and care for our homes and children comes from our desire to follow biblical precepts. When we obey God and keep His commands, we automatically gain a sense of servitude toward our family and others.

What's our duty? To love God and follow His will.

Let us hear the conclusion of the whole matter: Fear God, and keep his
commandments: for this is the whole duty of man.
ECCLESIASTES 12:13 KJV

If it is disagreeable in your sight to serve the LORD, choose
for yourselves today whom you will serve: whether the gods
which your fathers served which were beyond the River, or
the gods of the Amorites in whose land you are living; but
as for me and my house, we will serve the LORD.
JOSHUA 24:15 NASB

Now if you obey me fully and keep my covenant, then out of all nations you
will be my treasured possession. Although the whole earth is mine.
EXODUS 19:5 NIV

You shall therefore keep His statutes and His
commandments which I command you today, that it may
go well with you and with your children after you, and that
you may prolong your days in the land which the LORD your
God is giving you for all time.
DEUTERONOMY 4:40 NKJV

When people's lives please the LORD, even their enemies
are at peace with them.
PROVERBS 16:7 NLT

So why do you keep calling me "Lord, Lord!"
when you don't do what I say?
LUKE 6:46 NLT

And shewing mercy unto thousands of them that love me,
and keep my commandments.
EXODUS 20:6 KJV

Be careful to listen to all these words which I command you, so that it may be well with you and your sons after you forever, for you will be doing what is good and right in the sight of the LORD your God.

DEUTERONOMY 12:28 NASB

All men will hate you because of me, but he who stands firm to the end will be saved.

MATTHEW 10:22 NIV

See, I have set before you today life and good, death and evil, in that I command you today to love the LORD your God, to walk in His ways, and to keep His commandments, His statutes, and His judgments, that you may live and multiply; and the LORD your God will bless you in the land which you go to possess.

DEUTERONOMY 30:15–16 NKJV

*Laziness may appear attractive,
but work gives satisfaction.*

ANNE FRANK

Encouragement

A little encouragement goes a long way.
It's been a bad week. You lost your car keys, burned your favorite recipe, misplaced important papers, ran late for work, and forgot a parent-teacher conference. Plus, your devotional time seems to have disappeared with those keys.

Discouraged, you enter church on Sunday fully prepared to force a fake smile. Instead, you're encouraged. The Sunday school lesson and sermon are just for you and the fellowship is great. Instantly, your deflated optimism fades into the distant past and you are revitalized, ready to share the encouragement you received with someone else.

You must warn each other every day, while it is still "today," so that none of you will be deceived by sin and hardened against God.
HEBREWS 3:13 NLT

> Confirming the souls of the disciples, and exhorting them to continue in the faith, and that we must through much tribulation enter into the kingdom of God.
> ACTS 14:22 KJV

Holding fast the faithful word which is in accordance with the teaching, so that he will be able both to exhort in sound doctrine and to refute those who contradict.
TITUS 1:9 NASB

> Let us not give up meeting together, as some are in the habit of doing, but let us encourage one another— and all the more as you see the Day approaching.
> HEBREWS 10:25 NIV

I can do all things through Christ who strengthens me.
PHILIPPIANS 4:13 NKJV

> With all these things in mind, dear brothers and sisters, stand firm and keep a strong grip on the teaching we passed on to you both in person and by letter. Now may our Lord Jesus Christ himself and God our Father, who loved us and by his grace gave us eternal comfort and a wonderful hope, comfort you and strengthen you in every good thing you do and say.
> 2 THESSALONIANS 2:15–17 NLT

Therefore encourage one another and build each other up,
just as in fact you are doing.
1 Thessalonians 5:11 NIV

Now if we are afflicted, it is for your consolation and
salvation, which is effective for enduring the same sufferings
which we also suffer. Or if we are comforted,
it is for your consolation and salvation.
2 Corinthians 1:6 NKJV

Share each other's burdens, and in this way obey the law of Christ.
Galatians 6:2 NLT

Ye are witnesses, and God also, how holily and justly and
unblameably we behaved ourselves among you that
believe: as ye know how we exhorted and comforted and
charged every one of you, as a father doth his children,
that ye would walk worthy of God, who hath called you
unto his kingdom and glory. For this cause also thank we
God without ceasing, because, when ye received the
word of God which ye heard of us, ye received it not as the
word of men, but as it is in truth, the word of God, which
effectually worketh also in you that believe.
1 Thessalonians 2:10–13 KJV

Do not merely look out for your own personal interests,
but also for the interests of others.
Philippians 2:4 NASB

All Scripture is God-breathed and is useful for teaching,
rebuking, correcting and training in righteousness.
2 Timothy 3:16 NIV

Brethren, if anyone among you wanders from the truth, and someone turns him back, let him know that he who turns a sinner from the error of his way will save a soul from death and cover a multitude of sins.
JAMES 5:19–20 NKJV

When they bring you before the synagogues and the rulers and the authorities, do not worry about how or what you are to speak in your defense, or what you are to say; for the Holy Spirit will teach you in that very hour what you ought to say.
LUKE 12:11–12 NASB

What men and women need
is encouragement. . . .
Instead of always harping on
a man's faults, tell him of his virtues.
Try to pull him out of his
rut of bad habits.
ELEANOR H. PORTER

Eternity

$\mathcal{E}$arthly life is short but eternity is forever. With that in mind, we all need to stand ready to meet the Lord.

Heaven is an actual place, not some mystical golden-gated wisp of cumulus clouds topped with angels. The most majestic places, ideals, and valued treasures can't compare to what God has prepared for those who love Him. And the best part about heaven is the One who rules and reigns there.

Right now, Jesus prepares your eternal home. And one day all of life's problems and trials will vanish in the light of an eternity with Him.

There is more than enough room in my Father's home. If this were not so, would I have told you that I am going to prepare a place for you? When everything is ready, I will come and get you, so that you will always be with me where I am.
JOHN 14:2–3 NLT

> In the future there is laid up for me the crown of righteousness, which the Lord, the righteous Judge, will award to me on that day; and not only to me, but also to all who have loved His appearing.
> 2 TIMOTHY 4:8 NASB

And I saw a new heaven and a new earth: for the first heaven and the first earth were passed away; and there was no more sea. And I John saw the holy city, new Jerusalem, coming down from God out of heaven, prepared as a bride adorned for her husband.
REVELATION 21:1–2 KJV

> Jesus said to them, "You will indeed drink from my cup, but to sit at my right or left is not for me to grant. These places belong to those for whom they have been prepared by my Father."
> MATTHEW 20:23 NIV

And I give them eternal life, and they shall never perish; neither shall anyone snatch them out of My hand.
JOHN 10:28 NKJV

> Those who love their life in this world will lose it. Those who care nothing for their life in this world will keep it for eternity.
> JOHN 12:25 NLT

Behold, I tell you a mystery: We shall not all sleep, but we shall all be changed— in a moment, in the twinkling of an eye, at the last trumpet. For the trumpet will sound, and the dead will be raised incorruptible, and we shall be changed. For this corruptible must put on incorruption, and this mortal must put on immortality. So when this corruptible has put on incorruption, and this mortal has put on immortality, then shall be brought to pass the saying that is written: "Death is swallowed up in victory."
1 CORINTHIANS 15:51–54 NKJV

But in keeping with his promise we are looking forward to a new heaven and a new earth, the home of righteousness.
2 PETER 3:13 NIV

For he who sows to his flesh will of the flesh reap corruption, but he who sows to the Spirit will of the Spirit reap everlasting life.
GALATIANS 6:8 NKJV

And when the Great Shepherd appears, you will receive a crown of never-ending glory and honor.
1 PETER 5:4 NLT

And many of them that sleep in the dust of the earth shall awake, some to everlasting life, and some to shame and everlasting contempt.
DANIEL 12:2 KJV

Jesus said to her, "I am the resurrection and the life; he who believes in Me will live even if he dies, and everyone who lives and believes in Me will never die. Do you believe this?"
JOHN 11:25–26 NASB

You diligently study the Scriptures because you think that by them you possess eternal life. These are the Scriptures that testify about me.
JOHN 5:39 NIV

But in accordance with your hardness and your impenitent heart you are treasuring up for yourself wrath in the day of wrath and revelation of the righteous judgment of God, who "will render to each one according to his deeds": eternal life to those who by patient continuance in doing good seek for glory, honor, and immortality.
ROMANS 2:5–7 NKJV

But don't be so concerned about perishable things like food. Spend your energy seeking the eternal life that the Son of Man can give you. For God the Father has given me the seal of his approval.
JOHN 6:27 NLT

All praise to God, the Father of our Lord Jesus Christ. It is by his great mercy that we have been born again, because God raised Jesus Christ from the dead. Now we live with great expectation, and we have a priceless inheritance— an inheritance that is kept in heaven for you, pure and undefiled, beyond the reach of change and decay. And through your faith, God is protecting you by his power until you receive this salvation, which is ready to be revealed on the last day for all to see.
1 PETER 1:3–5 NLT

And there will no longer be any night; and they will not have need of the light of a lamp nor the light of the sun, because the Lord God will illumine them; and they will reign forever and ever.
REVELATION 22:5 NASB

But if the Spirit of him that raised up Jesus from the dead dwell in you, he that raised up Christ from the dead shall also quicken your mortal bodies by his Spirit that dwelleth in you.

ROMANS 8:11 KJV

Therefore are they before the throne of God, and serve him day and night in his temple: and he that sitteth on the throne shall dwell among them. They shall hunger no more, neither thirst any more; neither shall the sun light on them, nor any heat. For the Lamb which is in the midst of the throne shall feed them, and shall lead them unto living fountains of waters: and God shall wipe away all tears from their eyes.

REVELATION 7:15–17 KJV

*Redeemed,
how I love to proclaim it!
His child, and forever, I am.*

FANNIE CROSBY

Faith

You may be unaware of it, but you exercise faith daily. By faith you fall asleep, confident of morning. You eat, expecting nourishment. You breathe in air you can't see. You drive your car, trusting it will take you to your destination.

Jesus said that faith as tiny as a mustard seed is enough to produce miraculous results. So why do we assume that only mountain-moving faith will do? The Word of God is a faith-builder. So read on and cause that mustard seed to flourish and grow.

But he must ask in faith without any doubting, for the one who doubts is like the surf of the sea, driven and tossed by the wind.
JAMES 1:6 NASB

He replied, "If you have faith as small as a mustard seed, you can say to this mulberry tree, 'Be uprooted and planted in the sea,' and it will obey you."
LUKE 17:6 NIV

Whom having not seen, you love. Though now you do not see Him, yet believing, you rejoice with joy inexpressible and full of glory.
1 PETER 1:8 NKJV

But Jesus overheard them and said to Jairus, "Don't be afraid. Just have faith."
MARK 5:36 NLT

And he said to the woman, Thy faith hath saved thee; go in peace.
LUKE 7:50 KJV

For you are all sons of God through faith in Christ Jesus.
GALATIANS 3:26 NASB

Yet to all who received him, to those who believed in his name, he gave the right to become children of God.
JOHN 1:12 NIV

That Christ may dwell in your hearts by faith; that ye, being rooted and grounded in love, may be able to comprehend with all saints what is the breadth, and length, and depth, and height; and to know the love of Christ, which passeth knowledge, that ye might be filled with all the fulness of God.
EPHESIANS 3:17–19 KJV

And Jesus said to him, "'If You can?' All things are possible
to him who believes."
MARK 9:23 NASB

It is written in the Prophets: "They will all be taught by God."
Everyone who listens to the Father and learns from him
comes to me.
JOHN 6:45 NIV

That your faith should not be in the wisdom of men
but in the power of God.
1 CORINTHIANS 2:5 NKJV

Be on guard. Stand firm in the faith.
Be courageous. Be strong.
1 CORINTHIANS 16:13 NLT

That if thou shalt confess with thy mouth the Lord Jesus, and shalt believe
in thine heart that God hath raised him from the dead,
thou shalt be saved.
ROMANS 10:9 KJV

Jesus said to him, "Thomas, because you have seen Me,
you have believed. Blessed are those who have not seen
and yet have believed."
JOHN 20:29 NKJV

And it is impossible to please God without faith. Anyone who wants to
come to him must believe that God exists and that he rewards
those who sincerely seek him.
HEBREWS 11:6 NLT

For we walk by faith, not by sight.
2 CORINTHIANS 5:7 KJV

Jesus answered and said to them, "This is the work of God,
that you believe in Him whom He has sent."
JOHN 6:29 NASB

Behold, I stand at the door and knock. If anyone hears My
voice and opens the door, I will come in to him and dine
with him, and he with Me.
REVELATION 3:20 NKJV

Anyone who believes in the Son of God has this testimony in his heart. Anyone
who does not believe God has made him out to be a liar, because
he has not believed the testimony God has given about his Son.
1 JOHN 5:10 NIV

And now, just as you accepted Christ Jesus as your Lord,
you must continue to follow him. Let your roots grow down
into him, and let your lives be built on him. Then your faith
will grow strong in the truth you were taught,
and you will overflow with thankfulness.
COLOSSIANS 2:6–7 NLT

Let us draw near with a sincere heart in full assurance of faith, having our
hearts sprinkled clean from an evil conscience and our bodies
washed with pure water.
HEBREWS 10:22 NASB

Jesus saith unto her, Said I not unto thee, that, if thou
wouldest believe, thou shouldest see the glory of God?
JOHN 11:40 KJV

I have been crucified with Christ; and it is no longer I who live, but Christ lives in me; and the life which I now live in the flesh I live by faith in the Son of God, who loved me and gave Himself up for me.
GALATIANS 2:20 NASB

Faith sees the invisible, believes the unbelievable, and receives the impossible.

CORRIE TEN BOOM

Faithfulness of God

It's a fact. Even the most dependable people fail us: our husbands, our parents, our friends. They don't mean to—they're only human just as we are. On the other hand, we can fully depend on God's faithfulness at all times.

What God says, He does. His promises are true. What He did for His people and the prophets of old, He does for us today. We can safely trust Him at His Word whatever the circumstance. Always remember: God cannot lie, and His faithfulness endures forever.

It's a fact!

And we know that in all things God works for the good of those who love him,
who have been called according to his purpose.
ROMANS 8:28 NIV

And the heavens will praise Your wonders, O LORD;
Your faithfulness also in the assembly of the saints.
PSALM 89:5 NKJV

The trustworthy person will get a rich reward,
but a person who wants quick riches will get into trouble.
PROVERBS 28:20 NLT

In hope of eternal life, which God, that cannot lie,
promised before the world began.
TITUS 1:2 KJV

*Who then is the faithful and sensible slave whom his master put in charge of his
household to give them their food at the proper time?* Blessed is that slave
whom his master finds so doing when he comes. Truly I say to
you that he will put him in charge of all his possessions.
MATTHEW 24:45–47 NASB

So this is what the Sovereign LORD says: "See, I lay a stone
in Zion, a tested stone, a precious cornerstone for a sure
foundation; the one who trusts will never be dismayed."
ISAIAH 28:16 NIV

(For the LORD thy God is a merciful God;) he will not forsake thee,
neither destroy thee, nor forget the covenant of thy fathers
which he sware unto them.
DEUTERONOMY 4:31 KJV

> Let us hold fast the confession of our hope without
> wavering, for He who promised is faithful.
> HEBREWS 10:23 NASB

Do not be afraid of what you are about to suffer. I tell you, the devil
will put some of you in prison to test you, and you will suffer
persecution for ten days. Be faithful, even to the point of death,
and I will give you the crown of life.
REVELATION 2:10 NIV

> God is not a man, that He should lie, nor a son of man,
> that He should repent. Has He said, and will He not do?
> Or has He spoken, and will He not make it good?
> NUMBERS 23:19 NKJV

Praise the LORD who has given rest to his people Israel, just as he
promised. Not one word has failed of all the wonderful promises
he gave through his servant Moses.
1 KINGS 8:56 NLT

> O love the LORD, all ye his saints: for the LORD preserveth the
> faithful, and plentifully rewardeth the proud doer.
> PSALM 31:23 KJV

Know therefore that the LORD your God, He is God, the faithful
God, who keeps His covenant and His lovingkindness to a
thousandth generation with those who love Him and keep His
commandments.
DEUTERONOMY 7:9 NASB

If we are faithless, He remains faithful;
He cannot deny Himself.
2 TIMOTHY 2:13 NKJV

The Lord isn't really being slow about his promise, as some people think. No, he is being patient for your sake. He does not want anyone to be destroyed, but wants everyone to repent. 2 PETER 3:9 NLT

God's designs regarding you,
and His methods of bringing about
these designs, are infinitely wise.
MADAME GUYON

Fearing God

Fear God? Aren't we supposed to trust, not fear the Lord? Fear isn't of God, right?

In the following verses we discover the definition of "fearing" God, and it's not what some people might think. The word *fear* is derived from the Greek word *eulabeia*, signifying caution and reverence.

When a godly fear and love are combined, they constitute a heartfelt devotion toward God. To fear the Lord is to reverence, love, respect, and honor Him. There's nothing scary about that!

Do not be afraid of those who kill the body but cannot kill the soul. Rather, be afraid of the One who can destroy both soul and body in hell.
MATTHEW 10:28 NIV

Moreover you shall select from all the people able men, such as fear God, men of truth, hating covetousness; and place such over them to be rulers of thousands, rulers of hundreds, rulers of fifties, and rulers of tens.
EXODUS 18:21 NKJV

Fear of the LORD is the foundation of true knowledge, but fools despise wisdom and discipline.
PROVERBS 1:7 NLT

Saying with a loud voice, Fear God, and give glory to him; for the hour of his judgment is come: and worship him that made heaven, and earth, and the sea, and the fountains of waters.
REVELATION 14:7 KJV

Oh that they had such a heart in them, that they would fear Me and keep all My commandments always, that it may be well with them and with their sons forever!
DEUTERONOMY 5:29 NASB

The angel of the LORD encamps around those who fear him, and he delivers them.
PSALM 34:7 NIV

A wise man feareth, and departeth from evil: but the fool rageth, and is confident.
PROVERBS 14:16 KJV

Therefore, since we receive a kingdom which cannot be
shaken, let us show gratitude, by which we may offer to
God an acceptable service with reverence and awe;
for our God is a consuming fire.
HEBREWS 12:28–29 NASB

Therefore, men revere him, for does he not have regard
for all the wise in heart?
JOB 37:24 NIV

Therefore, my beloved, as you have always obeyed, not as
in my presence only, but now much more in my absence,
work out your own salvation with fear and trembling.
PHILIPPIANS 2:12 NKJV

Because we have these promises, dear friends, let us cleanse ourselves
from everything that can defile our body or spirit. And let us
work toward complete holiness because we fear God.
2 CORINTHIANS 7:1 NLT

He will fulfil the desire of them that fear him:
he also will hear their cry, and will save them.
PSALM 145:19 KJV

The secret of the LORD is with those who fear Him,
and He will show them His covenant.
PSALM 25:14 NKJV

Have you no respect for me? Why don't you tremble in my
presence? I, the LORD, define the ocean's sandy shoreline as
an everlasting boundary that the waters cannot cross.
The waves may toss and roar, but they can
never pass the boundaries I set.
JEREMIAH 5:22 NLT

Serve the LORD with fear, and rejoice with trembling.
PSALM 2:11 KJV

Then those who feared the LORD spoke to one another,
and the LORD gave attention and heard it, and a book of
remembrance was written before Him for those who fear
the LORD and who esteem His name.
MALACHI 3:16 NASB

Reverence for the Lord
is the beginning of wisdom.
ELISABETH ELLIOT

Forgiveness

How do we forgive someone who has wronged us or hurt someone we love? How can we forgive when we don't *feel* forgiveness?

Corrie ten Boom, survivor of a women's Nazi concentration camp, wrote: "Forgiveness is an act of the will, and the will can function regardless of the temperature of the heart."

For every Christian, forgiveness is a choice. In order to fully receive God's forgiveness we must willingly extend forgiveness to others.

Through an act of her will, Corrie forgave her persecutors and her sister's murderers. Jesus forgave humankind of even more. How can we do less?

Be kind and compassionate to one another, forgiving each other,
just as in Christ God forgave you.
EPHESIANS 4:32 NIV

Bearing with one another, and forgiving one another,
if anyone has a complaint against another;
even as Christ forgave you, so you also must do.
COLOSSIANS 3:13 NKJV

Don't repay evil for evil. Don't retaliate with insults when people
insult you. Instead, pay them back with a blessing. That is what
God has called you to do, and he will bless you for it.
1 PETER 3:9 NLT

For if ye forgive men their trespasses, your heavenly
Father will also forgive you: But if ye forgive not men their
trespasses, neither will your Father forgive your trespasses.
MATTHEW 6:14–15 KJV

Then Peter came and said to Him, "Lord, how often shall my brother
sin against me and I forgive him? Up to seven times?" Jesus said
to him, "I do not say to you, up to seven times,
but up to seventy times seven."
MATTHEW 18:21–22 NASB

So watch yourselves. If your brother sins, rebuke him,
and if he repents, forgive him. If he sins against you seven
times in a day, and seven times comes back to you
and says, "I repent," forgive him.
LUKE 17:3–4 NIV

And forgive us our sins; for we also forgive every one that is indebted to us. And lead us not into temptation; but deliver us from evil.
LUKE 11:4 KJV

But I say to you, do not resist an evil person; but whoever slaps you on your right cheek, turn the other to him also. If anyone wants to sue you and take your shirt, let him have your coat also. Whoever forces you to go one mile, go with him two.
MATTHEW 5:39–41 NASB

Forgive us our debts, as we also have forgiven our debtors.
MATTHEW 6:12 NIV

If My people who are called by My name will humble themselves, and pray and seek My face, and turn from their wicked ways, then I will hear from heaven, and will forgive their sin and heal their land.
2 CHRONICLES 7:14 NKJV

O Lord, you are so good, so ready to forgive,
so full of unfailing love for all who ask for your help.
PSALM 86:5 NLT

Judge not, and ye shall not be judged:
condemn not, and ye shall not be condemned:
forgive, and ye shall be forgiven.
LUKE 6:37 KJV

Turning toward the woman, He said to Simon, "Do you see this woman? I entered your house; you gave Me no water for My feet, but she has wet My feet with her tears and wiped them with her hair. You gave Me no kiss; but she, since the time I came in, has not ceased to kiss My feet. You did not anoint My head with oil, but she anointed My feet with perfume. For this reason I say to you, her sins, which are many, have been forgiven, for she loved much; but he who is forgiven little, loves little." Then He said to her, "Your sins have been forgiven."
LUKE 7:44–48 NASB

If the wounds of millions are to be healed, what other way is there except through forgiveness?
CATHERINE MARSHALL

Friendship

Society uses the term *friendship* loosely. Social networking Web sites like Facebook connect us with scores of "friends" simultaneously—yet many of them are only acquaintances, not true friends.

The following passages unveil the meaning of a true friend. She's someone who brings out the best in you, who loves and gives unselfishly. She listens and speaks the truth with kindness—and when others criticize you, she stands in your defense.

Friendship is never one-sided because to have a friend, we must be a friend. Think of your very best girlfriend. Does she reflect the attributes of a true friend? Do you?

As iron sharpens iron, so one man sharpens another.
PROVERBS 27:17 NIV

And He said to them, "Which of you shall have a friend, and go to him at midnight and say to him, 'Friend, lend me three loaves; for a friend of mine has come to me on his journey, and I have nothing to set before him'; and he will answer from within and say, 'Do not trouble me; the door is now shut, and my children are with me in bed; I cannot rise and give to you'? I say to you, though he will not rise and give to him because he is his friend, yet because of his persistence he will rise and give him as many as he needs."
LUKE 11:5–8 NKJV

A friend is always loyal, and a brother is born to help in time of need.
PROVERBS 17:17 NLT

A man that hath friends must shew himself friendly: and there is a friend that sticketh closer than a brother.
PROVERBS 18:24 KJV

For the despairing man there should be kindness from his friend; so that he does not forsake the fear of the Almighty.
JOB 6:14 NASB

My friends are my estate.
EMILY DICKINSON

Generosity

$\mathcal{E}$ach Thanksgiving, Phyllis opens her home to the widows and singles of her church. She spends hours in meal preparations and sets the table with her finest china and best linens. Becky spends eight hours each week babysitting for young moms in need of a break. And for years, Lori and Esther have visited a local nursing home, sharing small gifts and homemade cookies with the residents.

Displays of generosity are as varied and numerous as the human fingerprint. Giving of our time, money, or talents is generous because we are giving of ourselves.

They share freely and give generously to those in need. Their good deeds will be remembered forever. They will have influence and honor.
PSALM 112:9 NLT

Do not withhold good from those who deserve it, when it is in your power to act. Do not say to your neighbor, "Come back later; I'll give it tomorrow" —when you now have it with you.
PROVERBS 3:27–28 NIV

He answered and said to them, "He who has two tunics, let him give to him who has none; and he who has food, let him do likewise."
LUKE 3:11 NKJV

When you give to someone in need, don't do as the hypocrites do—blowing trumpets in the synagogues and streets to call attention to their acts of charity! I tell you the truth, they have received all the reward they will ever get. But when you give to someone in need, don't let your left hand know what your right hand is doing. Give your gifts in private, and your Father, who sees everything, will reward you.
MATTHEW 6:2–4 NLT

He that despiseth his neighbour sinneth: but he that hath mercy on the poor, happy is he.
PROVERBS 14:21 KJV

Now in case a countryman of yours becomes poor and his means with regard to you falter, then you are to sustain him, like a stranger or a sojourner, that he may live with you.
LEVITICUS 25:35 NASB

If any woman who is a believer has widows in her family, she should help them and not let the church be burdened with them, so that the church can help those widows who are really in need.
1 TIMOTHY 5:16 NIV

And He saw also a certain poor widow putting in two mites. So He said, "Truly I say to you that this poor widow has put in more than all; for all these out of their abundance have put in offerings for God, but she out of her poverty put in all the livelihood that she had."
LUKE 21:2–4 NKJV

There will always be some in the land who are poor. That is why I am commanding you to share freely with the poor and with other Israelites in need.
DEUTERONOMY 15:11 NLT

If a brother or sister be naked, and destitute of daily food, and one of you say unto them, Depart in peace, be ye warmed and filled; notwithstanding ye give them not those things which are needful to the body; what doth it profit?
JAMES 2:15–16 KJV

How blessed is he who considers the helpless; The LORD will deliver him in a day of trouble. The LORD will protect him and keep him alive, and he shall be called blessed upon the earth; and do not give him over to the desire of his enemies.
PSALM 41:1–2 NASB

Each man should give what he has decided in his heart to give, not reluctantly or under compulsion, for God loves a cheerful giver.
2 CORINTHIANS 9:7 NIV

Then the King will say to those on His right hand, "Come, you blessed of My Father, inherit the kingdom prepared for you from the foundation of the world: for I was hungry and you gave Me food; I was thirsty and you gave Me drink; I was a stranger and you took Me in; I was naked and you clothed Me; I was sick and you visited Me; I was in prison and you came to Me." Then the righteous will answer Him, saying, "Lord, when did we see You hungry and feed You, or thirsty and give You drink? When did we see You a stranger and take You in, or naked and clothe You? Or when did we see You sick, or in prison, and come to You?" And the King will answer and say to them, "Assuredly, I say to you, inasmuch as you did it to one of the least of these My brethren, you did it to Me."
MATTHEW 25:34–40 NKJV

Share your food with the hungry, and give shelter to the homeless. Give clothes to those who need them, and do not hide from relatives who need your help. Then your salvation will come like the dawn, and your wounds will quickly heal. Your godliness will lead you forward, and the glory of the LORD will protect you from behind.
ISAIAH 58:7–8 NLT

For whosoever shall give you a cup of water to drink in my name, because ye belong to Christ, verily I say unto you, he shall not lose his reward.
MARK 9:41 KJV

Give, and it will be given to you: good measure, pressed down, shaken together, and running over will be put into your bosom. For with the same measure that you use, it will be measured back to you.
LUKE 6:38 NKJV

If you help the poor, you are lending to the LORD—
and he will repay you!
PROVERBS 19:17 NLT

I have shewed you all things, how that so labouring
ye ought to support the weak, and to remember the
words of the Lord Jesus, how he said, It is more blessed
to give than to receive.
ACTS 20:35 KJV

It's not how much we give
but how much love
we put into
giving.
MOTHER TERESA

Gentleness

Dr. James Dobson, Christian psychologist and author, recalls the gentleness his wife exhibited whenever she awakened their then-small daughter from a nap. Standing nearby, Dobson would watch as Shirley gently stirred their child from slumber with her soft, sweet, soothing words. Her genteel manner impacted the renowned psychologist so much that he spoke of it many years later.

How we approach people matters. Are we brazen and critical? Or are we compassionate, seasoning our words with kindness? Gentleness is a fruit of the Spirit that brings much-needed relief in a harsh world.

Take My yoke upon you and learn from Me, for I am gentle and humble in heart, and you will find rest for your souls.
MATTHEW 11:29 NASB

But the meek will inherit the land and enjoy great peace.
PSALM 37:11 NIV

Now I, Paul, myself am pleading with you by the meekness and gentleness of Christ—who in presence am lowly among you, but being absent am bold toward you.
2 CORINTHIANS 10:1 NKJV

Remind the believers to submit to the government and its officers. They should be obedient, always ready to do what is good. They must not slander anyone and must avoid quarreling. Instead, they should be gentle and show true humility to everyone.
TITUS 3:1–2 NLT

He tends his flock like a shepherd: He gathers the lambs in his arms and carries them close to his heart; he gently leads those that have young.
ISAIAH 40:11 NIV

He leads the humble in justice, and He teaches the humble His way.
PSALM 25:9 NASB

But the fruit of the Spirit is love, joy, peace, longsuffering, gentleness, goodness, faith.
GALATIANS 5:22 KJV

For the LORD taketh pleasure in his people:
he will beautify the meek with salvation.

PSALM 149:4 KJV

But the wisdom from above is first pure, then peaceable, gentle,
reasonable, full of mercy and good fruits,
unwavering, without hypocrisy.
JAMES 3:17 NASB

The LORD sustains the humble but casts
the wicked to the ground.

PSALM 147:6 NIV

You have also given me the shield of Your salvation;
Your gentleness has made me great.
2 SAMUEL 22:36 NKJV

As apostles of Christ we certainly had a right to make some
demands of you, but instead we were like children among
you. Or we were like a mother feeding
and caring for her own children.

1 THESSALONIANS 2:7 NLT

*Take my heart and make it
your dwelling place
so that everyone I touch
will be touched also by you!*

ALICE JOYCE DAVIDSON

God's Love

Have you ever read 1 Corinthians 13—the "Love Chapter"? The Living Bible says that love is patient and kind; never boastful, selfish, or rude. Love never demands its own way or is glad about injustice—rather, love rejoices when the truth wins out. Love is loyal no matter the cost. Love always believes the best in us and stands its ground in defending us.

Now substitute the word *love* with "God" and read that paragraph again. You see, God not only loves—He *is* love. No other love in heaven or on earth compares to God's because His very nature defines *agape*—selfless, unconditional—love. And that's how God loves us.

Behold, what manner of love the Father hath bestowed upon us, that we should be called the sons of God.
1 JOHN 3:1 KJV

By this the love of God was manifested in us, that God has sent His only begotten Son into the world so that we might live through Him.
1 JOHN 4:9 NASB

I will heal their waywardness and love them freely, for my anger has turned away from them.
HOSEA 14:4 NIV

But as it is written: "Eye has not seen, nor ear heard, nor have entered into the heart of man the things which God has prepared for those who love Him."
1 CORINTHIANS 2:9 NKJV

And I am convinced that nothing can ever separate us from God's love. Neither death nor life, neither angels nor demons, neither our fears for today nor our worries about tomorrow—not even the powers of hell can separate us from God's love. No power in the sky above or in the earth below—indeed, nothing in all creation will ever be able to separate us from the love of God that is revealed in Christ Jesus our Lord.
ROMANS 8:38–39 NLT

And hope maketh not ashamed; because the love of God is shed abroad in our hearts by the Holy Ghost which is given unto us.
ROMANS 5:5 KJV

The Lord preserves all who love Him, but all the wicked He will destroy.
Psalm 145:20 NKJV

For God loved the world so much that he gave his one and
only Son, so that everyone who believes in him
will not perish but have eternal life.
John 3:16 NLT

But God commendeth his love toward us, in that, while we were yet
sinners, Christ died for us.
Romans 5:8 KJV

For the Father Himself loves you, because you have loved
Me and have believed that I came forth from the Father.
John 16:27 NASB

*Love has its source in God,
for love is the very essence of His being.*

Kay Arthur

God's Provision

In recent years, a failing economy has caused much distress. People have lost their jobs and homes, and parents wonder how they will support their families. Yet it doesn't take a job loss to experience a financial drain, resulting in a shortage of basic necessities.

The following scriptures encourage us with words of hope and promise. Every Christian has the assurance of God's provision during tough times. As we wisely manage our money and trust in His promises, the Lord supplies—perhaps not our wants—but every one of our needs.

The lions may grow weak and hungry, but those who seek the Lord lack no good thing.
Psalm 34:10 niv

And my God shall supply all your need according to
His riches in glory by Christ Jesus.
Philippians 4:19 nkjv

He gives food to those who fear him; he always remembers his covenant.
Psalm 111:5 nlt

For this reason I say to you, do not be worried about your life, as to what you will eat or what you will drink; nor for your body, as to what you will put on. Is not life more than food, and the body more than clothing? Look at the birds of the air, that they do not sow, nor reap nor gather into barns, and yet your heavenly Father feeds them. Are you not worth much more than they? And who of you by being worried can add a single hour to his life? And why are you worried about clothing? Observe how the lilies of the field grow; they do not toil nor do they spin, yet I say to you that not even Solomon in all his glory clothed himself like one of these. But if God so clothes the grass of the field, which is alive today and tomorrow is thrown into the furnace, will He not much more clothe you? You of little faith! Do not worry then, saying, "What will we eat?" or "What will we drink?" or "What will we wear for clothing?" For the Gentiles eagerly seek all these things; for your heavenly Father knows that you need all these things. But seek first His kingdom and His righteousness, and all these things will be added to you.
Matthew 6:25–33 nasb

Charge them that are rich in this world, that they be not highminded,
nor trust in uncertain riches, but in the living God,
who giveth us richly all things to enjoy.
1 TIMOTHY 6:17 KJV

Once I was young, and now I am old. Yet I have never seen
the godly abandoned or their children begging for bread.
PSALM 37:25 NLT

Lift up your eyes.
Your heavenly Father waits
to bless you in inconceivable ways
to make your life what you never
dreamed it could be.
ANNE ORTLUND

Gratitude

$\mathcal{E}$vangelist Joyce Meyer has said, "Christians need an attitude of gratitude!"

Though we know that God frowns on murmuring and complaining, we do it anyway. We grumble about long stoplights, difficult neighbors, the weather, our jobs, family members, or household chores. Instead of thanking God for our blessings, we approach life with resignation rather than anticipation and gratefulness.

But what if we adjusted our attitude? We might just be happy! God's Word motivates us to discover and maintain a thankful spirit. Try it! Seize an attitude of gratitude.

Then he took the cup, gave thanks and offered it to them, saying, "Drink from it, all of you."
MATTHEW 26:27 NIV

I will praise You, O LORD, with my whole heart; I will tell of all Your marvelous works. I will be glad and rejoice in You; I will sing praise to Your name, O Most High.
PSALM 9:1–2 NKJV

Singing a song of thanksgiving and telling of all your wonders.
PSALM 26:7 NLT

Blessed be the LORD, that hath given rest unto his people Israel, according to all that he promised: there hath not failed one word of all his good promise, which he promised by the hand of Moses his servant.
1 KINGS 8:56 KJV

O LORD, You have brought up my soul from Sheol; You have kept me alive, that I would not go down to the pit.
PSALM 30:3 NASB

He who regards one day as special, does so to the Lord. He who eats meat, eats to the Lord, for he gives thanks to God; and he who abstains, does so to the Lord and gives thanks to God.
ROMANS 14:6 NIV

And they, continuing daily with one accord in the temple, and breaking bread from house to house, did eat their meat with gladness and singleness of heart, praising God, and having favour with all the people. And the Lord added to the church daily such as should be saved.
ACTS 2:46–47 KJV

Many, O Lord my God, are the wonders which You have done, and Your thoughts toward us; there is none to compare with You. If I would declare and speak of them, they would be too numerous to count.

PSALM 40:5 NASB

I will tell of the kindnesses of the LORD, the deeds for which he is to be praised, according to all the LORD has done for us— yes, the many good things he has done for the house of Israel, according to his compassion and many kindnesses.

ISAIAH 63:7 NIV

Blessed be the Lord, who daily loads us with benefits, the God of our salvation! Selah.

PSALM 68:19 NKJV

I thank and praise you, God of my ancestors, for you have given me wisdom and strength. You have told me what we asked of you and revealed to us what the king demanded.

DANIEL 2:23 NLT

In every thing give thanks: for this is the will of God in Christ Jesus concerning you.

1 THESSALONIANS 5:18 KJV

Give thanks to the LORD, for He is good, for His lovingkindness is everlasting.

PSALM 136:1 NASB

Then he took the seven loaves and the fish, and when he had given thanks, he broke them and gave them to the disciples, and they in turn to the people.

MATTHEW 15:36 NIV

It is good to give thanks to the LORD, and to sing praises to Your name, O Most High; to declare Your lovingkindness in the morning, and Your faithfulness every night.

PSALM 92:1–2 NKJV

Simple gratitude helps us
experience God
at work in every moment
of every day.

HARRIET CROSBY

Honesty

The cashier gives you too much money in change. Do you tell her? Out-of-town friends call unexpectedly and ask to stop by. Your house is a mess, you're dead tired, and you're in your pajamas. What do you say?

These scenarios happen all the time, giving us an opportunity to shine with honesty or dim with deceit. God's Word tells us to be aboveboard and upright in our dealings with others.

The old adage says, "Honesty is the best policy." Yet it's more than that. Honesty is a way of life.

And now, dear brothers and sisters, one final thing. Fix your thoughts on what is true, and honorable, and right, and pure, and lovely, and admirable. Think about things that are excellent and worthy of praise.
PHILIPPIANS 4:8 NLT

> Servants, obey in all things your masters according to the flesh; not with eyeservice, as menpleasers; but in singleness of heart, fearing God.
> COLOSSIANS 3:22 KJV

You shall not steal, nor deal falsely, nor lie to one another.
LEVITICUS 19:11 NASB

> The night is nearly over; the day is almost here. So let us put aside the deeds of darkness and put on the armor of light. Let us behave decently, as in the daytime, not in orgies and drunkenness, not in sexual immorality and debauchery, not in dissension and jealousy.
> ROMANS 13:12–13 NIV

Pray for us; for we are confident that we have a good conscience, in all things desiring to live honorably.
HEBREWS 13:18 NKJV

> Make it your goal to live a quiet life, minding your own business and working with your hands, just as we instructed you before. Then people who are not Christians will respect the way you live, and you will not need to depend on others.
> 1 THESSALONIANS 4:11–12 NLT

Be of the same mind one toward another. . . . Recompense to no man evil for evil. Provide things honest in the sight of all men.
ROMANS 12:16–17 KJV

> Do not lie to one another, since you laid aside the old self with its evil practices, and have put on the new self who is being renewed to a true knowledge according to the image of the One who created him.
> COLOSSIANS 3:9–10 NASB

For we are taking pains to do what is right, not only in the eyes of the Lord but also in the eyes of men.
2 CORINTHIANS 8:21 NIV

> He who does not put out his money at usury, nor does he take a bribe against the innocent. He who does these things shall never be moved.
> PSALM 15:5 NKJV

Because of this, I always try to maintain a clear conscience before God and all people.
ACTS 24:16 NLT

> Thou knowest the commandments, Do not commit adultery, Do not kill, Do not steal, Do not bear false witness.
> MARK 10:19 KJV

He that hath clean hands, and a pure heart; who hath not lifted up his soul unto vanity, nor sworn deceitfully.
PSALM 24:4 KJV

Make room for us in your hearts; we wronged no one, we corrupted no one, we took advantage of no one.
2 CORINTHIANS 7:2 NASB

He who walks righteously and speaks with sincerity, he who rejects unjust gain and shakes his hands so that they hold no bribe; he who stops his ears from hearing about bloodshed and shuts his eyes from looking upon evil; he will dwell on the heights, his refuge will be the impregnable rock; his bread will be given him, his water will be sure.
ISAIAH 33:15–16 NASB

Even corrupt tax collectors came to be baptized and asked, "Teacher, what should we do?" He replied, "Collect no more taxes than the government requires."
LUKE 3:12–13 NLT

I will maintain my righteousness and never let go of it; my conscience will not reproach me as long as I live.
JOB 27:6 NIV

Do not do what you would undo if caught.
LEAH ARENDT

Honor

To honor is to highly esteem someone for their integrity, honesty, uprightness, or courage. We pay homage to our veterans for their service to our country; we laud athletes, students, entertainers, ministers, and others who achieve excellence in their fields. In other words, we honor people we value and deem worthy of our respect.

The below verses tell us to honor the Lord with our tithes, our adoration, and everything we have. Far above all others, God is worthy of *all* our honor and praise.

Honor the Lord with your possessions,
and with the firstfruits of all your increase.
PROVERBS 3:9 NKJV

Children, obey your parents because you belong to the
Lord, for this is the right thing to do. "Honor your father and
mother." This is the first commandment with a promise:
If you honor your father and mother, "things will go well
for you, and you will have a long life on the earth."
EPHESIANS 6:1–3 NLT

She is more precious than jewels; and nothing you desire compares
with her. Long life is in her right hand; in her left hand
are riches and honor.
PROVERBS 3:15–16 NASB

Honour thy father and thy mother: that thy days may be
long upon the land which the LORD thy God giveth thee.
EXODUS 20:12 KJV

*Let our actions make us
worthy of the blessing we
have received and [pray] that
God will continue
to bless us!*

DIANE ALBERS

Hope

Have you ever hoped for something? Maybe a bigger house? A smaller dress size? A day to yourself? Or maybe more serious things like a physical healing or restoration of your marriage?

The word *hope* in the Greek translation is *elpis*, meaning "confident expectation in the unseen future" or "the happy expectation of good."

Hope launches a positive outlook. Without it, lives remain fragmented and broken, personal dreams go unrealized, and sick hearts lose the capacity to cope. Hope tells you to hold on in anticipation and expectation—because something good is just ahead!

For I know the thoughts that I think toward you, says the LORD,
thoughts of peace and not of evil, to give you a future and a hope.
JEREMIAH 29:11 NKJV

Dear friends, we are already God's children, but he has not
yet shown us what we will be like when Christ appears.
But we do know that we will be like him, for we will see
him as he really is. And all who have this eager
expectation will keep themselves pure, just as he is pure.
1 JOHN 3:2–3 NLT

And not only so, but we glory in tribulations also: knowing that
tribulation worketh patience; and patience, experience;
and experience, hope: And hope maketh not ashamed.
ROMANS 5:3–5 KJV

The hope of the righteous is gladness,
but the expectation of the wicked perishes.
PROVERBS 10:28 NASB

Praise be to the God and Father of our Lord Jesus Christ!
In his great mercy he has given us new birth into a living hope
through the resurrection of Jesus Christ from the dead.
1 PETER 1:3 NIV

Blessed is the man who trusts in the LORD,
and whose hope is the LORD.
JEREMIAH 17:7 NKJV

"The LORD is my portion," says my soul, "Therefore I have hope in Him." The LORD is good to those who wait for Him, to the person who seeks Him. It is good that he waits silently for the salvation of the LORD.
LAMENTATIONS 3:24–26 NASB

> But since we belong to the day, let us be self-controlled, putting on faith and love as a breastplate, and the hope of salvation as a helmet.
> 1 THESSALONIANS 5:8 NIV

My soul faints for Your salvation, but I hope in Your word.
PSALM 119:81 NKJV

> Instead, you must worship Christ as Lord of your life. And if someone asks about your Christian hope, always be ready to explain it.
> 1 PETER 3:15 NLT

In hope of eternal life, which God, that cannot lie, promised before the world began.
TITUS 1:2 KJV

> For we through the Spirit, by faith, are waiting for the hope of righteousness.
> GALATIANS 5:5 NASB

But Christ is faithful as a son over God's house. And we are his house, if we hold on to our courage and the hope of which we boast.
HEBREWS 3:6 NIV

That by two immutable things, in which it is impossible for
God to lie, we might have strong consolation, who have
fled for refuge to lay hold of the hope set before us.
This hope we have as an anchor of the soul, both sure and
steadfast, and which enters the Presence behind the veil.
HEBREWS 6:18–19 NKJV

I pray that God, the source of hope, will fill you completely with joy
and peace because you trust in him. Then you will overflow with
confident hope through the power of the Holy Spirit.
ROMANS 15:13 NLT

To whom God would make known what is the riches of the
glory of this mystery among the Gentiles;
which is Christ in you, the hope of glory.
COLOSSIANS 1:27 KJV

Who through Him are believers in God, who raised Him from the dead
and gave Him glory, so that your faith and hope are in God.
1 PETER 1:21 NASB

And I have the same hope in God as these men, that there
will be a resurrection of both the righteous and the wicked.
ACTS 24:15 NIV

And we desire that each one of you show the same diligence to
the full assurance of hope until the end.
HEBREWS 6:11 NKJV

There is one body and one Spirit,
just as also you were called in one hope of your calling.
EPHESIANS 4:4 NASB

For in this hope we were saved. But hope that is seen is no hope at all. Who hopes for what he already has? But if we hope for what we do not yet have, we wait for it patiently.
ROMANS 8:24–25 NIV

LORD, I hope for Your salvation,
and I do Your commandments.
PSALM 119:166 NKJV

Since this new way gives us such confidence, we can be very bold.
2 CORINTHIANS 3:12 NLT

The eyes of your understanding being enlightened;
that ye may know what is the hope of his calling,
and what the riches of the glory of his inheritance in the saints.
EPHESIANS 1:18 KJV

According to my earnest expectation and hope, that I will not be put to shame in anything, but that with all boldness,
Christ will even now, as always, be exalted in my body,
whether by life or by death.
PHILIPPIANS 1:20 NASB

Remember your word to your servant,
for you have given me hope.
PSALM 119:49 NIV

Why are you cast down, O my soul? And why are you disquieted within me? Hope in God; for I shall yet praise Him, the help of my countenance and my God.
PSALM 42:11 NKJV

Which come from your confident hope of what God has reserved for you in heaven. You have had this expectation ever since you first heard the truth of the Good News.
COLOSSIANS 1:5 NLT

Looking for that blessed hope, and the glorious appearing of the great God and our Saviour Jesus Christ.
TITUS 2:13 KJV

Now faith is the assurance of things hoped for, the conviction of things not seen.
HEBREWS 11:1 NASB

But the needy will not always be forgotten,
nor the hope of the afflicted ever perish.
PSALM 9:18 NIV

Optimism is the faith
that leads to achievement.
Nothing can be done without
hope and confidence.
HELEN KELLER

Hospitality

Women and hospitality go together like coffee and cream. Generally, women are the ones who host family gatherings, church dinners, kids' birthday parties, and so much more.

Back in the 1930s and '40s, vagabonds would often go house-to-house for food. Without hesitation, the woman of the house would serve the stranger a hot meal. Of course, that kind of hospitality is dangerous today. Yet we should continue to open our homes and give to those we *do* know.

After all, a hospitable woman not only opens her home, she opens her heart.

Do not forget to entertain strangers, for by so doing some have unwittingly entertained angels.
HEBREWS 13:2 NKJV

> Do not take advantage of foreigners who live among you in your land. Treat them like native-born Israelites, and love them as you love yourself. Remember that you were once foreigners living in the land of Egypt. I am the LORD your God.
> LEVITICUS 19:33–34 NLT

Use hospitality one to another without grudging.
1 PETER 4:9 KJV

> For the overseer must be above reproach as God's steward, not self-willed, not quick-tempered, not addicted to wine, not pugnacious, not fond of sordid gain, but hospitable, loving what is good, sensible, just, devout, self-controlled.
> TITUS 1:7–8 NASB

Wisdom has built her house; she has hewn out its seven pillars. She has prepared her meat and mixed her wine; she has also set her table. She has sent out her maids, and she calls from the highest point of the city. "Let all who are simple come in here!" she says to those who lack judgment. "Come, eat my food and drink the wine I have mixed."
PROVERBS 9:1–5 NIV

> Distributing to the needs of the saints, given to hospitality.
> ROMANS 12:13 NKJV

Instead, invite the poor, the crippled, the lame, and the blind. Then at the resurrection of the righteous, God will reward you for inviting those who could not repay you.
LUKE 14:13–14 NLT

Well reported of for good works; if she have brought up children, if she have lodged strangers, if she have washed the saints' feet, if she have relieved the afflicted, if she have diligently followed every good work.
1 TIMOTHY 5:10 KJV

Nor shall you glean your vineyard, nor shall you gather the fallen fruit of your vineyard; you shall leave them for the needy and for the stranger. I am the LORD your God.
LEVITICUS 19:10 NASB

Suppose a brother or sister is without clothes and daily food. If one of you says to him, "Go, I wish you well; keep warm and well fed," but does nothing about his physical needs, what good is it?
JAMES 2:15–16 NIV

Then the King will say to those on His right hand, "Come, you blessed of My Father, inherit the kingdom prepared for you from the foundation of the world: for I was hungry and you gave Me food; I was thirsty and you gave Me drink; I was a stranger and you took Me in; I was naked and you clothed Me; I was sick and you visited Me; I was in prison and you came to Me." And the King will answer and say to them, "Assuredly, I say to you, inasmuch as you did it to one of the least of these My brethren, you did it to Me."
MATTHEW 25:34–36, 40 NKJV

He ensures that orphans and widows receive justice.
He shows love to the foreigners living among you
and gives them food and clothing.
DEUTERONOMY 10:18 NLT

For whosoever shall give you a cup of water to drink in my name,
because ye belong to Christ, verily I say unto you,
he shall not lose his reward.
MARK 9:41 KJV

Just allow your guest to feel at ease
because you are, whatever the
state of your house.
This is an important element
to being a gracious host.
LINDA DAVIS ZUMBEHL

Humility

Nineteenth-century missionary Mary Slessor said: "Blessed is the man or woman who is able to serve cheerfully in the second rank—a big test."

Serving in the limelight is one thing, but serving absent of accolades and applause is another. Those who take a backseat and work as hard as if they were in the front seat are diligent. But those who take a backseat and have no thought of taking credit for their deeds are humble.

Jesus said, "The first shall be last and the last shall be first" in God's kingdom. Humility leads to greatness, and great people are the ones who are humble.

Be of the same mind toward one another; do not be haughty in mind, but associate with the lowly. Do not be wise in your own estimation.
ROMANS 12:16 NASB

This is what the LORD says: "Let not the wise man boast of his wisdom or the strong man boast of his strength or the rich man boast of his riches."
JEREMIAH 9:23 NIV

If I must boast, I will boast in the things which concern my infirmity.
2 CORINTHIANS 11:30 NKJV

Don't brag about tomorrow, since you don't know what the day will bring.
PROVERBS 27:1 NLT

Whosoever therefore shall humble himself as this little child, the same is greatest in the kingdom of heaven.
MATTHEW 18:4 KJV

When you are cast down, you will speak with confidence, and the humble person He will save.
JOB 22:29 NASB

Young men, in the same way be submissive to those who are older. All of you, clothe yourselves with humility toward one another, because, "God opposes the proud but gives grace to the humble." Humble yourselves, therefore, under God's mighty hand, that he may lift you up in due time.
1 PETER 5:5–6 NIV

LORD, my heart is not haughty, nor mine eyes lofty:
neither do I exercise myself in great matters,
or in things too high for me.

PSALM 131:1 KJV

Blessed are the poor in spirit, for theirs is the kingdom of heaven.
MATTHEW 5:3 NASB

Listen to me, you who pursue righteousness and who seek
the LORD: Look to the rock from which you were cut and to
the quarry from which you were hewn.

ISAIAH 51:1 NIV

LORD, You have heard the desire of the humble; You will prepare their
heart; You will cause Your ear to hear.
PSALM 10:17 NKJV

The LORD mocks the mockers but is gracious to the humble.
PROVERBS 3:34 NLT

And whosoever shall exalt himself shall be abased; and he that shall
humble himself shall be exalted.
MATTHEW 23:12 KJV

But made Himself of no reputation, taking the form of a
bondservant, and coming in the likeness of men. And being
found in appearance as a man, He humbled Himself and
became obedient to the point of death, even the death
of the cross. Therefore God also has highly exalted Him and
given Him the name which is above every name.

PHILIPPIANS 2:7–9 NKJV

Pride leads to disgrace, but with humility comes wisdom.
PROVERBS 11:2 NLT

For though the LORD is exalted, yet He regards the lowly,
but the haughty He knows from afar.
PSALM 138:6 NASB

For this is what the high and lofty One says—he who lives forever, whose name is holy: "I live in a high and holy place, but also with him who is contrite and lowly in spirit, to revive the spirit of the lowly and to revive the heart of the contrite."
ISAIAH 57:15 NIV

When he maketh inquisition for blood, he remembereth
them: he forgetteth not the cry of the humble.
PSALM 9:12 KJV

Humble yourselves in the presence of the Lord, and He will exalt you.
JAMES 4:10 NASB

All of the charm and beauty a woman may
have amounts to nothing if her ambitions are
self-centered. But if she reflects her Creator
and assumes the posture of a graceful
servant, she cannot help but
command high respect and love.

JEANNE HENDRICKS

Joy

Do you know someone who has a spirit of joy? No matter what happens in life, she always has an uplifting word and a glowing smile. She sparkles with joy brighter than polished diamonds and, not surprisingly, everyone enjoys her company.

The scriptures encourage us to delight in the Lord that way—to illuminate with joy about our salvation and the goodness of God. Our joy should shine in such a way that it lights the pathway to lead others to Christ.

One day, we will rejoice in heaven. That fact alone should cause us to jump for joy!

But the angel reassured them. "Don't be afraid!" he said. "I bring you good news that will bring great joy to all people."
LUKE 2:10 NLT

The LORD is my strength and my shield; my heart trusted in him, and I am helped: therefore my heart greatly rejoiceth; and with my song will I praise him.
PSALM 28:7 KJV

Rejoice in the Lord always; again I will say, rejoice!
PHILIPPIANS 4:4 NASB

Until now you have not asked for anything in my name. Ask and you will receive, and your joy will be complete.
JOHN 16:24 NIV

Be glad in the LORD and rejoice, you righteous; and shout for joy, all you upright in heart!
PSALM 32:11 NKJV

Evil people are trapped by sin, but the righteous escape, shouting for joy.
PROVERBS 29:6 NLT

As sorrowful, yet always rejoicing; as poor, yet making many rich; as having nothing, and yet possessing all things.
2 CORINTHIANS 6:10 KJV

So the ransomed of the LORD shall return, and come to Zion with singing, with everlasting joy on their heads. They shall obtain joy and gladness; sorrow and sighing shall flee away.
ISAIAH 51:11 NKJV

The master was full of praise. "Well done, my good and faithful servant. You have been faithful in handling this small amount, so now I will give you many more responsibilities. Let's celebrate together!"
MATTHEW 25:21 NLT

> Rejoice ye in that day, and leap for joy: for, behold, your reward is great in heaven: for in the like manner did their fathers unto the prophets.
> LUKE 6:23 KJV

Shout joyfully to the LORD, all the earth. Serve the LORD with gladness; come before Him with joyful singing.
PSALM 100:1–2 NASB

> I am coming to you now, but I say these things while I am still in the world, so that they may have the full measure of my joy within them.
> JOHN 17:13 NIV

All the days of the afflicted are evil, but he who is of a merry heart has a continual feast.
PROVERBS 15:15 NKJV

> Not that we lord it over your faith, but are workers with you for your joy; for in your faith you are standing firm.
> 2 CORINTHIANS 1:24 NASB

Is any one of you in trouble? He should pray. Is anyone happy? Let him sing songs of praise.
JAMES 5:13 NIV

For our heart shall rejoice in Him,
because we have trusted in His holy name.

PSALM 33:21 NKJV

Singing psalms and hymns and spiritual songs among yourselves,
and making music to the Lord in your hearts.

EPHESIANS 5:19 NLT

I will greatly rejoice in the LORD, my soul shall be joyful
in my God; for he hath clothed me with the garments
of salvation, he hath covered me with the robe of
righteousness, as a bridegroom decketh himself with
ornaments,and as a bride adorneth herself with her jewels.

ISAIAH 61:10 KJV

Laughter lightens the load.

PATSY CLAIRMONT

Kindness

*Y*ears ago, Oprah Winfrey encouraged her audience to engage in "random acts of kindness." She led the crusade through personal example with deeds such as paying the toll for the person in the vehicle behind her. Her message was simple: Extend one act of kindness to a stranger each day.

Kindness is rooted in a giving heart. The virtue is displayed in small ways like driving an elderly patient to the doctor, cooking a meal for a shut-in, babysitting for a busy mom, or simply sharing a smile.

When kindness is the rule, there's nothing random about it.

Give to everyone who asks of you, and whoever takes away what is yours, do not demand it back.
LUKE 6:30 NASB

Do not repay evil with evil or insult with insult, but with blessing, because to this you were called so that you may inherit a blessing.
1 PETER 3:9 NIV

She opens her mouth with wisdom, and on her tongue is the law of kindness.
PROVERBS 31:26 NKJV

Since God chose you to be the holy people he loves, you must clothe yourselves with tenderhearted mercy, kindness, humility, gentleness, and patience.
COLOSSIANS 3:12 NLT

And to godliness brotherly kindness; and to brotherly kindness charity. For if these things be in you, and abound. . .ye shall neither be barren nor unfruitful in the knowledge of our Lord Jesus Christ.
2 PETER 1:7–8 KJV

Each of us is to please his neighbor for his good, to his edification.
ROMANS 15:2 NASB

This is what the LORD Almighty says: "Administer true justice; show mercy and compassion to one another. Do not oppress the widow or the fatherless, the alien or the poor. In your hearts do not think evil of each other."
ZECHARIAH 7:9–10 NIV

But in everything commending ourselves as servants of
God, in much endurance, in afflictions, in hardships,
in distresses. . .in purity, in knowledge, in patience,
in kindness, in the Holy Spirit, in genuine love. . .as sorrowful
yet always rejoicing, as poor yet making many rich,
as having nothing yet possessing all things.
2 CORINTHIANS 6:4, 6, 10 NASB

Be happy with those who are happy, and weep with those who weep.
ROMANS 12:15 NLT

As we have therefore opportunity, let us do good unto all
men, especially unto them who are of
the household of faith.
GALATIANS 6:10 KJV

He who despises his neighbor sins,
but happy is he who is gracious to the poor.
PROVERBS 14:21 NASB

Give to the one who asks you, and do not turn away from
the one who wants to borrow from you.
MATTHEW 5:42 NIV

He can have compassion on those who are ignorant and going astray,
since he himself is also subject to weakness.
HEBREWS 5:2 NKJV

The desire of a man is his kindness: and a poor man is better
than a liar. The fear of the LORD tendeth to life: and he that
hath it shall abide satisfied.
PROVERBS 19:22–23 KJV

"The LORD bless you, my daughter!" Boaz exclaimed. "You are showing even more family loyalty now than you did before, for you have not gone after a younger man, whether rich or poor. Now don't worry about a thing, my daughter. I will do what is necessary, for everyone in town knows you are a virtuous woman."
RUTH 3:10–11 NLT

Let no one ever come to you without
leaving better and happier.
Be the living expression of God's kindness:
kindness in your face,
kindness in your eyes,
kindness in your smile.
MOTHER TERESA

Love of God

Do you love God? Some would think that a trick question. Of course every Christian loves God! Don't they?

The following scriptures address this subject. They tell us that if we love God we will—among other things—seek Him and keep His commandments. Placing God first and desiring His will above our own demonstrates our love and devotion to the One who has done, and continues to do, so much for us.

Loving God is more than lip service, it's God-service.

The LORD watches over all who love him, but all the wicked he will destroy.
PSALM 145:20 NIV

Therefore take careful heed to yourselves,
that you love the LORD your God.
JOSHUA 23:11 NKJV

Understand, therefore, that the LORD your God is indeed God. He is the
faithful God who keeps his covenant for a thousand generations
and lavishes his unfailing love on those who love him
and obey his commands.
DEUTERONOMY 7:9 NLT

And Jesus answered him, The first of all the commandments
is, Hear, O Israel; The Lord our God is one Lord: And thou
shalt love the Lord thy God with all thy heart, and with all
thy soul, and with all thy mind, and with all thy strength:
this is the first commandment. And the second is like,
namely this, Thou shalt love thy neighbour as thyself.
There is none other commandment greater than these.
MARK 12:29–31 KJV

That Christ may dwell in your hearts through faith; that you, being rooted
and grounded in love, may be able to comprehend with all the
saints what is the width and length and depth and height—
to know the love of Christ which passes knowledge;
that you may be filled with all the fullness of God.
EPHESIANS 3:17–19 NKJV

Jesus told them, "If God were your Father, you would love
me, because I have comes to you from God.
I am not here on my own, but he sent me."
JOHN 8:42 NLT

For God is not unrighteous to forget your work and labour of love,
which ye have shewed toward his name.
HEBREWS 6:10 KJV

You shall love the LORD your God with all your heart and with
all your soul and with all your might.
DEUTERONOMY 6:5 NASB

Do not love the world or anything in the world. If anyone loves the world,
the love of the Father is not in him.
1 JOHN 2:15 NIV

I love those who love me, and those who seek me
diligently will find me.
PROVERBS 8:17 NKJV

Take delight in the LORD, and he will give you your heart's desires.
PSALM 37:4 NLT

And we know that all things work together for good to
them that love God, to them who are the called
according to his purpose.
ROMANS 8:28 KJV

I will declare Your name to My brethren;
in the midst of the assembly I will praise You.
PSALM 22:22 NKJV

And await the mercy of our Lord Jesus Christ,
who will bring you eternal life. In this way,
you will keep yourselves safe in God's love.
JUDE 21 NLT

And we have known and believed the love that God hath to us. God is love; and he that dwelleth in love dwelleth in God, and God in him. Herein is our love made perfect, that we may have boldness in the day of judgment: because as he is, so are we in this world. There is no fear in love; but perfect love casteth out fear: because fear hath torment. He that feareth is not made perfect in love. We love him, because he first loved us.
1 JOHN 4:16–19 KJV

He who has My commandments and keeps them is the one who loves Me; and he who loves Me will be loved by My Father, and I will love him and will disclose Myself to him.
JOHN 14:21 NASB

The greatest need in the world today is love. . .
More love for each other and more love for God above!
HELEN STEINER RICE

Love for Others

God commands us to love others, and guess what? That includes our enemies, too.

It's easy to love those who love us or—at the very least—to love those who are somewhat lovable. But our enemies?

Enemy is a strong word, but you get the picture. It describes anyone who is hostile or adversarial toward you. Like the coworker who diminishes your job position while aggrandizing hers. Or the neighbor who persistently gossips about you despite your efforts to help her.

God's love compels us to love, forgive, understand, and pray for one another. . .even the unlovable.

Be devoted to one another in brotherly love.
Honor one another above yourselves.
ROMANS 12:10 NIV

But concerning brotherly love you have no need that I
should write to you, for you yourselves are taught
by God to love one another.
1 THESSALONIANS 4:9 NKJV

For the whole law can be summed up in this one command:
"Love your neighbor as yourself."
GALATIANS 5:14 NLT

And to godliness brotherly kindness;
and to brotherly kindness charity.
2 PETER 1:7 KJV

Beloved, if God so loved us, we also ought to love one another. No one has
seen God at any time; if we love one another, God abides in us,
and His love is perfected in us.
1 JOHN 4:11–12 NASB

And now these three remain: faith, hope and love.
But the greatest of these is love.
1 CORINTHIANS 13:13 NIV

Thou shalt not avenge, nor bear any grudge against the children of
thy people, but thou shalt love thy neighbour as thyself:
I am the LORD.
LEVITICUS 19:18 KJV

If I speak with the tongues of men and of angels, but do not have love, I have become a noisy gong or a clanging cymbal. If I have the gift of prophecy, and know all mysteries and all knowledge; and if I have all faith, so as to remove mountains, but do not have love, I am nothing. And if I give all my possessions to feed the poor, and if I surrender my body to be burned, but do not have love, it profits me nothing.

1 Corinthians 13:1–3 NASB

Let no debt remain outstanding, except the continuing debt to love one another, for he who loves his fellowman has fulfilled the law.
Romans 13:8 NIV

And because of your knowledge shall the weak brother perish, for whom Christ died? But when you thus sin against the brethren, and wound their weak conscience, you sin against Christ.

1 Corinthians 8:11–12 NKJV

Let us think of ways to motivate one another to acts of love and good works.
Hebrews 10:24 NLT

In this the children of God are manifest, and the children of the devil: whosoever doeth not righteousness is not of God, neither he that loveth not his brother.

1 John 3:10 KJV

I say this to your shame. Is it so, that there is not a wise man among you, not even one, who will be able to judge between his brethren? But brother goes to law against brother, and that before unbelievers! Now therefore, it is already an utter failure for you that you go to law against one another. Why do you not rather accept wrong? Why do you not rather let yourselves be cheated? No, you yourselves do wrong and cheat, and you do these things to your brethren!
1 CORINTHIANS 6:5–8 NKJV

If someone says, "I love God," but hates a Christian brother or sister, that person is a liar; for if we don't love people we can see, how can we love God, whom we cannot see? And he has given us this command: Those who love God must also love their Christian brothers and sisters.
1 JOHN 4:20–21 NLT

Leave there thy gift before the altar, and go thy way; first be reconciled to thy brother, and then come and offer thy gift.
MATTHEW 5:24 KJV

Since you have in obedience to the truth purified your souls for a sincere love of the brethren, fervently love one another from the heart.
1 PETER 1:22 NASB

A new commandment I give to you, that you love one another, even as I have loved you, that you also love one another. By this all men will know that you are My disciples, if you have love for one another.
JOHN 13:34–35 NASB

Dear friends, let us love one another, for love comes from God. Everyone who loves has been born of God and knows God. Whoever does not love does not know God, because God is love. This is how God showed his love among us: He sent his one and only Son into the world that we might live through him. This is love: not that we loved God, but that he loved us and sent his Son as an atoning sacrifice for our sins. Dear friends, since God so loved us, we also ought to love one another.

1 John 4:7–11 niv

Finally, all of you be of one mind, having compassion for one another; love as brothers, be tenderhearted, be courteous.
1 Peter 3:8 nkjv

If I put my own good name before the other's highest good, then I know nothing of Calvary love.

Amy Carmichael

Meekness

How can a Type-A lady, with an exuberant, take-charge, outgoing personality, exhibit meekness? Wouldn't that contradict who she really is?

Jesus not only encourages meekness in His beatitudes, He described Himself as "meek and lowly in heart" (Matthew 11:29 KJV). Yet Jesus was no pushover.

Meekness isn't our outward behavior, but an inwrought grace of the soul. It is a tempered spirit fully surrendered to God, one that accepts His dealings without dispute or resistance. Meekness demonstrates full devotion to and humility before God.

Jesus said that the meek will inherit the earth. And that includes Type-A personalities, too.

The poor will eat and be satisfied. All who seek the LORD will praise him. Their hearts will rejoice with everlasting joy.
PSALM 22:26 NLT

> Great is our Lord, and of great power: his understanding is infinite. The LORD lifteth up the meek: he casteth the wicked down to the ground.
> PSALM 147:5–6 KJV

The afflicted also will increase their gladness in the LORD, and the needy of mankind will rejoice in the Holy One of Israel.
ISAIAH 29:19 NASB

> Wives, in the same way be submissive to your husbands so that, if any of them do not believe the word, they may be won over without words by the behavior of their wives. . . . Your beauty should not come from outward adornment, such as braided hair and the wearing of gold jewelry and fine clothes. Instead, it should be that of your inner self, the unfading beauty of a gentle and quiet spirit, which is of great worth in God's sight.
> 1 PETER 3:1, 3–4 NIV

Seek the LORD, all you meek of the earth, who have upheld His justice. Seek righteousness, seek humility. It may be that you will be hidden in the day of the LORD's anger.
ZEPHANIAH 2:3 NKJV

> Blessed are the gentle, for they shall inherit the earth.
> MATTHEW 5:5 NASB

Good and upright is the LORD; therefore he instructs sinners in his ways. He guides the humble in what is right and teaches them his way.
PSALM 25:8–9 NIV

Take my yoke upon you, and learn of me; for I am meek and lowly in heart: and ye shall find rest unto your souls.
MATTHEW 11:29 KJV

Brethren, if a man is overtaken in any trespass, you who are spiritual restore such a one in a spirit of gentleness, considering yourself lest you also be tempted. Bear one another's burdens, and so fulfill the law of Christ.
GALATIANS 6:1–2 NKJV

For the LORD delights in his people; he crowns the humble with victory.
PSALM 149:4 NLT

We can do no great things;
only small things with great love.
MOTHER TERESA

Mercy

God is merciful. If He wasn't, most of us would be in big trouble!

The Greek translation of *mercy* means "an outward manifestation of pity; it assumes need on the part of him who receives it, and the resources adequate to meet the need on the part of him who shows it."

If we love when wronged, we show mercy. If we give or forgive despite our grievances, we exhibit mercy. And if we understand those who are misunderstood, we are merciful.

Teamed with goodness, mercy shall follow believers all the days of their lives (Psalm 23:6). Lord, have mercy!

Be ye therefore merciful, as your Father also is merciful.
LUKE 6:36 KJV

But You, O Lord, are a God merciful and gracious, slow to
anger and abundant in lovingkindness and truth.
PSALM 86:15 NASB

But you must return to your God; maintain love and justice,
and wait for your God always.
HOSEA 12:6 NIV

Blessed are the merciful, for they shall obtain mercy.
MATTHEW 5:7 NKJV

We give great honor to those who endure under suffering. For instance,
you know about Job, a man of great endurance. You can see
how the Lord was kind to him at the end, for the Lord
is full of tenderness and mercy.
JAMES 5:11 NLT

For thou, Lord, art good, and ready to forgive;
and plenteous in mercy unto all them that call upon thee.
PSALM 86:5 KJV

He has told you, O man, what is good; and what does the LORD require
of you but to do justice, to love kindness, and to walk humbly
with your God?
MICAH 6:8 NASB

For God has imprisoned everyone in disobedience so he
could have mercy on everyone.
ROMANS 11:32 NLT

The LORD is good to all: and his tender mercies are over all his works.
PSALM 145:9 KJV

Do not let kindness and truth leave you; bind them around your neck, write them on the tablet of your heart. So you will find favor and good repute in the sight of God and man.
PROVERBS 3:3–4 NASB

He who conceals his sins does not prosper, but whoever confesses and renounces them finds mercy.
PROVERBS 28:13 NIV

But God, who is rich in mercy, because of His great love with which He loved us, even when we were dead in trespasses, made us alive together with Christ (by grace you have been saved).
EPHESIANS 2:4–5 NKJV

He saved us, not because of the righteous things we had done, but because of his mercy. He washed away our sins, giving us a new birth and new life through the Holy Spirit. He generously poured out the Spirit upon us through Jesus Christ our Savior. Because of his grace he declared us righteous and gave us confidence that we will inherit eternal life.
TITUS 3:5–7 NLT

Let the wicked forsake his way, and the unrighteous man his thoughts: and let him return unto the LORD, and he will have mercy upon him; and to our God, for he will abundantly pardon.
ISAIAH 55:7 KJV

"For I will be merciful to their iniquities, and I will remember their sins no more." When He said, "A new covenant," He has made the first obsolete. But whatever is becoming obsolete and growing old is ready to disappear.
HEBREWS 8:12–13 NASB

His mercy extends to those who fear him,
from generation to generation.
LUKE 1:50 NIV

Mercy and truth have met together; righteousness and peace have kissed.
PSALM 85:10 NKJV

Surely goodness and mercy shall follow me all the days of
my life: and I will dwell in the house of the LORD for ever.
PSALM 23:6 KJV

God deals with us from a merciful posture;
His arms are open, His words are healing,
He wants sinners to return to Him.

MARTIE STOWELL

Modesty

What is true modesty? Current fashions often expose too much skin or fit too tightly, but God's Word tells every woman to dress appropriately. What we wear and how we wear it matters to God because it reflects our inner character and spirit.

Modesty, however, goes far beyond the superficial. A modest spirit is clothed in humility and holiness. A woman who exhibits modesty is not boastful—rather, she seasons her words with kindness and grace. Doing otherwise brings her more embarrassment than wearing her pajamas in public!

And I want women to be modest in their appearance. They should wear decent and appropriate clothing and not draw attention to themselves by the way they fix their hair or by wearing gold or pearls or expensive clothes. For women who claim to be devoted to God should make themselves attractive by the good things they do.
1 TIMOTHY 2:9–10 NLT

Let no man deceive himself. If any man among you seemeth to be wise in this world, let him become a fool, that he may be wise.
1 CORINTHIANS 3:18 KJV

A man's pride will bring him low,
but a humble spirit will obtain honor.
PROVERBS 29:23 NASB

A woman with a gentle and quiet spirit
is not only precious to God, but she is
attractive to others also. She dresses
appropriately, but it is her inner adornment
that is noted because she is secure
and at rest within her spirit.
CYNTHIA HEALD

Obedience

*E*lisabeth Elliot, wife of martyred missionary Jim Elliot, said: "God is God. Because He is God, He is worthy of my trust and obedience."

A successful Christian walk is based on our obedience to Christ. In fact, to obey God is to love, serve, trust, and believe Him.

Consider how it pleases you when your child obeys you without question or resistance. He or she simply trusts you at your word and does what you ask. Nice, huh? The same is true of our heavenly Father. It pleases Him when we trust Him enough to obey.

Now then, if you will indeed obey My voice and keep My covenant,
then you shall be My own possession among all the peoples,
for all the earth is Mine.
EXODUS 19:5 NASB

Be careful to obey all these regulations I am giving you,
so that it may always go well with you and your children
after you, because you will be doing what is good and right
in the eyes of the LORD your God.
DEUTERONOMY 12:28 NIV

*You shall therefore keep His statutes and His commandments which I command
you today,* that it may go well with you and with your children after
you, and that you may prolong your days in the land which the
LORD your God is giving you for all time.
DEUTERONOMY 4:40 NKJV

My child, never forget the things I have taught you.
Store my commands in your heart. If you do this,
you will live many years, and your life will be satisfying.
PROVERBS 3:1–2 NLT

But whoso looketh into the perfect law of liberty, and continueth therein,
he being not a forgetful hearer, but a doer of the work, this man
shall be blessed in his deed.
JAMES 1:25 KJV

The things you have learned and received and heard and
seen in me, practice these things,
and the God of peace will be with you.
PHILIPPIANS 4:9 NASB

If they obey and serve him, they will spend the rest of their days in prosperity and their years in contentment.
JOB 36:11 NIV

Not everyone who calls out to me, "Lord! Lord!" will enter the Kingdom of Heaven. Only those who actually do the will of my Father in heaven will enter.
MATTHEW 7:21 NLT

In that I command you today to love the LORD your God, to walk in His ways, and to keep His commandments, His statutes, and His judgments, that you may live and multiply; and the LORD your God will bless you in the land which you go to possess.
DEUTERONOMY 30:16 NKJV

Let us hear the conclusion of the whole matter: Fear God, and keep his commandments: for this is the whole duty of man.
ECCLESIASTES 12:13 KJV

If you keep My commandments, you will abide in My love; just as I have kept My Father's commandments and abide in His love.
JOHN 15:10 NASB

So if you ignore the least commandment and teach others to do the same, you will be called the least in the Kingdom of Heaven. But anyone who obeys God's laws and teaches them will be called great in the Kingdom of Heaven.
MATTHEW 5:19 NLT

For not the hearers of the law are just before God, but the doers of the law shall be justified.
ROMANS 2:13 KJV

The world is passing away, and also its lusts;
but the one who does the will of God lives forever.
1 JOHN 2:17 NASB

He replied, "Blessed rather are those who hear
the word of God and obey it."
LUKE 11:28 NIV

Therefore keep the words of this covenant,
and do them, that you may prosper in all that you do.
DEUTERONOMY 29:9 NKJV

Since we respected our earthly fathers who disciplined us, shouldn't we
submit even more to the discipline of the Father of our spirits,
and live forever?
HEBREWS 12:9 NLT

Blessed are they that keep his testimonies,
and that seek him with the whole heart.
PSALM 119:2 KJV

So then, my beloved, just as you have always obeyed,
not as in my presence only, but now much more in my absence,
work out your salvation with fear and trembling.
PHILIPPIANS 2:12 NASB

If you are willing and obedient,
you will eat the best from the land.
ISAIAH 1:19 NIV

The only way I will keep a pliable,
obedient spirit
in the larger decisions
is to look to Him and to obey
in the smaller ones.

CATHERINE MARSHALL

Patience

Patience is a lost virtue in today's fast-paced, I-want-it-now society. We want results and we want them immediately! Just ask any woman on a diet. After a week or so, some of us fall off the wagon when the number on the scale doesn't drop quickly enough.

Our impatience surfaces in other ways, too—everything from waiting in a store checkout line to waiting for answered prayer.

Attaining patience is a process, often birthed from endurance on the battlefield of trials. Yet patience is a virtue worth working—and waiting—for.

And a servant of the Lord must not quarrel but be gentle to all,
able to teach, patient.
2 TIMOTHY 2:24 NKJV

Be still in the presence of the LORD, and wait patiently for him
to act. Don't worry about evil people who prosper or fret
about their wicked schemes. Stop being angry! Turn from
your rage! Do not lose your temper—it only leads to harm.
For the wicked will be destroyed, but those who
trust in the LORD will possess the land.
PSALM 37:7–9 NLT

For ye have need of patience, that, after ye have done the will of God,
ye might receive the promise.
HEBREWS 10:36 KJV

Here is the perseverance of the saints who keep the
commandments of God and their faith in Jesus.
REVELATION 14:12 NASB

Because you know that the testing of your faith develops perseverance.
Perseverance must finish its work so that you may be mature
and complete, not lacking anything.
JAMES 1:3–4 NIV

But the ones that fell on the good ground are those who,
having heard the word with a noble and good heart,
keep it and bear fruit with patience.
LUKE 8:15 NKJV

For whatever things were written before were written for our learning, that we through the patience and comfort of the Scriptures might have hope. Now may the God of patience and comfort grant you to be like-minded toward one another, according to Christ Jesus.
ROMANS 15:4–5 NKJV

May the Lord lead your hearts into a full understanding and expression of the love of God and the patient endurance that comes from Christ.
2 THESSALONIANS 3:5 NLT

In your patience possess ye your souls.
LUKE 21:19 KJV

Therefore be patient, brethren, until the coming of the Lord. The farmer waits for the precious produce of the soil, being patient about it, until it gets the early and late rains. You too be patient; strengthen your hearts, for the coming of the Lord is near.
JAMES 5:7–8 NASB

Therefore, since we are surrounded by such a great cloud of witnesses, let us throw off everything that hinders and the sin that so easily entangles, and let us run with perseverance the race marked out for us.
HEBREWS 12:1 NIV

That you do not become sluggish, but imitate those who through faith and patience inherit the promises.
HEBREWS 6:12 NKJV

Of course, you get no credit for being patient if you are beaten for doing wrong. But if you suffer for doing good and endure it patiently, God is pleased with you.
1 PETER 2:20 NLT

Better is the end of a thing than the beginning thereof:
and the patient in spirit is better than the proud in spirit.
Be not hasty in thy spirit to be angry:
for anger resteth in the bosom of fools.
ECCLESIASTES 7:8–9 KJV

And so, having patiently waited, he obtained the promise.
HEBREWS 6:15 NASB

To those who by persistence in doing good seek glory,
honor and immortality, he will give eternal life.
ROMANS 2:7 NIV

Obedience is the fruit of faith;
patience, the bloom
on the fruit.
CHRISTINA ROSSETTI

Peace

....

How do you describe peace? A day spent at the beach? An afternoon without phone calls and to-do lists? How about a stress-free week? Those things may initiate peace, but they are rarely the source of it.

God gives us a peace that surpasses human understanding—the kind of peace that prevails in the most difficult situations or alarming circumstances. Only the Lord can administer tranquility in the midst of life's storms.

Need peace? Relax and bask in the peace that only God provides.

For the mountains shall depart and the hills be removed, but My kindness shall not depart from you, nor shall My covenant of peace be removed, says the LORD, who has mercy on you. All your children shall be taught by the LORD, and great shall be the peace of your children.
ISAIAH 54:10, 13 NKJV

I pray that God, the source of hope, will fill you completely with joy and peace because you trust in him. Then you will overflow with confident hope through the power of the Holy Spirit.
ROMANS 15:13 NLT

The LORD will give strength unto his people; the LORD will bless his people with peace.
PSALM 29:11 KJV

When a man's ways are pleasing to the LORD, he makes even his enemies to be at peace with him.
PROVERBS 16:7 NASB

Blessed are the peacemakers, for they will be called sons of God.
MATTHEW 5:9 NIV

Deceit is in the heart of those who devise evil, but counselors of peace have joy.
PROVERBS 12:20 NKJV

And those who are peacemakers will plant seeds of peace and reap a harvest of righteousness.
JAMES 3:18 NLT

Do all that you can to live in peace with everyone.
ROMANS 12:18 NLT

And He will judge between the nations, and will render decisions
for many peoples; and they will hammer their swords into
plowshares and their spears into pruning hooks. Nation will not
lift up sword against nation, and never again will they learn war.
ISAIAH 2:4 NASB

And the peace of God, which passeth all understanding,
shall keep your hearts and minds through Christ Jesus.
PHILIPPIANS 4:7 KJV

Hold them in the highest regard in love because of their work.
Live in peace with each other.
1 THESSALONIANS 5:13 NIV

Therefore I exhort first of all that supplications, prayers,
intercessions, and giving of thanks be made for all men,
for kings and all who are in authority, that we may lead a
quiet and peaceable life in all godliness and reverence.
1 TIMOTHY 2:1–2 NKJV

Work at living in peace with everyone, and work at living a holy life,
for those who are not holy will not see the Lord.
HEBREWS 12:14 NLT

Behold, how good and how pleasant it is for brethren to
dwell together in unity!
PSALM 133:1 KJV

For, "the one who desires life, to love and see good days, must keep his tongue from evil and his lips from speaking deceit. He must turn away from evil and do good; he must seek peace and pursue it."
1 PETER 3:10–11 NASB

You will keep in perfect peace him whose mind is steadfast, because he trusts in you.
ISAIAH 26:3 NIV

For God has not given us a spirit of fear, but of power and of love and of a sound mind.
2 TIMOTHY 1:7 NKJV

I am leaving you with a gift—peace of mind and heart. And the peace I give is a gift the world cannot give. So don't be troubled or afraid.
JOHN 14:27 NLT

When the presence of the Lord really becomes your experience, you will actually discover that you have gradually begun to love this silence and peaceful rest which come with His presence.
MADAME GUYON

Perseverance

You've tried everything to no avail. Now what? You've prayed for a loved one for years, but nothing changes. What do you do?

The Lord tells us that after we've done everything we know to do, and have said everything we know to say, to stand. In other words, persevere. Keep believing, praying, and standing in faith.

The same holds true for every area of our lives. We must hold steady in the face of adversity, doubt, or apparent failure. Why? Because God is faithful if we will only stand fast and persevere against all odds.

For the which cause I also suffer these things: nevertheless I am not ashamed: for I know whom I have believed, and am persuaded that he is able to keep that which I have committed unto him against that day. Hold fast the form of sound words, which thou hast heard of me, in faith and love which is in Christ Jesus.
2 Timothy 1:12–13 kjv

> He who has an ear, let him hear what the Spirit says to the churches. He who overcomes will not be hurt by the second death.
> Revelation 2:11 nasb

We have come to share in Christ if we hold firmly till the end the confidence we had at first.
Hebrews 3:14 niv

> To him who overcomes I will grant to sit with Me on My throne, as I also overcame and sat down with My Father on His throne.
> Revelation 3:21 nkjv

These trials will show that your faith is genuine. It is being tested as fire tests and purifies gold—though your faith is far more precious than mere gold. So when your faith remains strong through many trials, it will bring you much praise and glory and honor on the day when Jesus Christ is revealed to the whole world.
1 Peter 1:7 nlt

> Thou therefore endure hardness, as a good soldier of Jesus Christ.
> 2 Timothy 2:3 kjv

Though he fall, he shall not be utterly cast down;
for the Lord upholds him with His hand.
PSALM 37:24 NKJV

Let us hold tightly without wavering to the hope we affirm,
for God can be trusted to keep his promise.
HEBREWS 10:23 NLT

For I am persuaded, that neither death, nor life, nor angels, nor
principalities, nor powers, nor things present, nor things to
come, nor height, nor depth, nor any other creature, shall be
able to separate us from the love of God, which is in
Christ Jesus our Lord.
ROMANS 8:38–39 KJV

It was for freedom that Christ set us free;
therefore keep standing firm and do not
be subject again to a yoke of slavery.
GALATIANS 5:1 NASB

The path of the righteous is like the first gleam of dawn,
shining ever brighter till the full light of day.
PROVERBS 4:18 NIV

Then Jesus said to those Jews who believed Him,
"If you abide in My word, you are My disciples indeed."
JOHN 8:31 NKJV

I am warning you ahead of time, dear friends. Be on guard so that you
will not be carried away by the errors of these wicked people and
lose your own secure footing.
2 PETER 3:17 NLT

Who shall separate us from the love of Christ?
Shall trouble or hardship or persecution or famine
or nakedness or danger or sword?
ROMANS 8:35 NIV

Therefore take up the whole armor of God, that you may be able to
withstand in the evil day, and having done all, to stand.
EPHESIANS 6:13 NKJV

Therefore, since we are surrounded by such a huge crowd
of witnesses to the life of faith, let us strip off every weight
that slows us down, especially the sin that so easily trips us
up. And let us run with endurance the race God has set
before us. We do this by keeping our eyes on Jesus,
the champion who initiates and perfects our faith.
Because of the joy awaiting him, he endured the cross,
disregarding its shame. Now he is seated in
the place of honor beside God's throne.
HEBREWS 12:1–2 NLT

Therefore, my brethren dearly beloved and longed for, my joy and crown,
so stand fast in the Lord, my dearly beloved.
PHILIPPIANS 4:1 KJV

*You may have to fight a battle
more than once to win it.*

MARGARET THATCHER

Power

....

Workshops, conferences, books, and magazines all herald the attributes of *empowerment* and what it can mean in a woman's life. We long to fortify ourselves with the knowledge, wisdom, capabilities, and tools that will give us the power to become or do something greater than ourselves.

The scriptures talk a lot about power, too—the power of God. As the Lord empowers us through the Holy Spirit, we change in ways we never dreamed and accomplish the seemingly impossible with His help. The truth is, self-empowerment often fades into futility, but God's power empowers the powerless continually.

Seek the LORD and His strength; seek His face continually.
1 CHRONICLES 16:11 NASB

The LORD your God is with you, he is mighty to save. He will take great delight in you, he will quiet you with his love, he will rejoice over you with singing.
ZEPHANIAH 3:17 NIV

Now to Him who is able to do exceedingly abundantly above all that we ask or think, according to the power that works in us.
EPHESIANS 3:20 NKJV

For the Kingdom of God is not just a lot of talk; it is living by God's power.
1 CORINTHIANS 4:20 NLT

The stone still stood there in that quiet garden, a reminder of the reality of the problem we all must live with; but Christ had moved it to one side so very easily, demonstrating His resurrection power on our behalf.

JILL BRISCOE

Prayer

A mother prays for her child at the foot of a tear-stained bed. An elderly woman sits in a wheelchair interceding for her church. A grandmother kneels at the kitchen sink to pray for her grandchildren. A young woman sits in a classroom, whispering a prayer for a friend, and a little girl places her hand on her sick puppy and prays.

Prayer is simply talking to God. Lofty words and pious phrases are unnecessary—only a pure, honest, and sincere heart matters. God's power is unleashed through prayer. So pray often, anywhere, anytime.

At that time you won't need to ask me for anything. I tell you the truth, you will ask the Father directly, and he will grant your request because you use my name. You haven't done this before. Ask, using my name, and you will receive, and you will have abundant joy.
JOHN 16:23–24 NLT

> But thou, when thou prayest, enter into thy closet, and when thou hast shut thy door, pray to thy Father which is in secret; and thy Father which seeth in secret shall reward thee openly. But when ye pray, use not vain repetitions, as the heathen do: for they think that they shall be heard for their much speaking.
> MATTHEW 6:6–7 KJV

Give ear to my words, O LORD, consider my groaning. Heed the sound of my cry for help, my King and my God, for to You I pray.
PSALM 5:1–2 NASB

> And will give our attention to prayer and the ministry of the word.
> ACTS 6:4 NIV

If you then, being evil, know how to give good gifts to your children, how much more will your Father who is in heaven give good things to those who ask Him!
MATTHEW 7:11 NKJV

> Rejoice in our confident hope.
> Be patient in trouble, and keep on praying.
> ROMANS 12:12 NLT

Pray continually.
1 THESSALONIANS 5:17 NIV

You will make your prayer to Him, He will hear you,
and you will pay your vows.
JOB 22:27 NKJV

Pray in the Spirit at all times and on every occasion. Stay alert and be
persistent in you prayers for all believers everywhere.
EPHESIANS 6:18 NLT

I waited patiently for the LORD;
and he inclined unto me, and heard my cry.
PSALM 40:1 KJV

Now, will not God bring about justice for His elect who cry to Him day and
night, and will He delay long over them?
LUKE 18:7 NASB

If my people, who are called by my name, will humble
themselves and pray and seek my face and turn from their
wicked ways, then will I hear from heaven and will forgive
their sin and will heal their land.
2 CHRONICLES 7:14 NIV

Then you will call upon Me and go and pray to Me, and I will listen to
you. And you will seek Me and find Me, when you search for Me
with all your heart.
JEREMIAH 29:12–13 NKJV

You can pray for anything, and if you have faith,
you will receive it.
MATTHEW 21:22 NLT

The Lord is nigh unto all them that call upon him, to all that call upon him in truth.
PSALM 145:18 KJV

Let us therefore come boldly unto the throne of grace, that we may obtain mercy, and find grace to help in time of need.
HEBREWS 4:16 KJV

The sacrifice of the wicked is an abomination to the LORD, but the prayer of the upright is His delight.
PROVERBS 15:8 NASB

Ask and it will be given to you; seek and you will find; knock and the door will be opened to you. For everyone who asks receives; he who seeks finds; and to him who knocks, the door will be opened.
MATTHEW 7:7–8 NIV

It shall come to pass that before they call, I will answer; and while they are still speaking, I will hear.
ISAIAH 65:24 NKJV

Confess your sins to each other and pray for each other so that you may be healed. The earnest prayer of a righteous person has great power and produces wonderful results.
JAMES 5:16 NLT

I want men everywhere to lift up holy hands in prayer, without anger or disputing.
1 TIMOTHY 2:8 NIV

Oh, that men would give thanks to the LORD
for His goodness, and for His wonderful works
to the children of men!
PSALM 107:15 NKJV

Well then, what shall I do? I will pray in the spirit, and I will also
pray in words I understand. I will sing in the spirit,
and I will also sing in words I understand.
1 CORINTHIANS 14:15 NLT

Yet the LORD will command his lovingkindness in the daytime,
and in the night his song shall be with me,
and my prayer unto the God of my life.
PSALM 42:8 KJV

Again I say to you, that if two of you agree on earth about anything that
they may ask, it shall be done for them by My Father who is in
heaven. For where two or three have gathered together in
My name, I am there in their midst.
MATTHEW 18:19–20 NASB

They caused the cry of the poor to come before him,
so that he heard the cry of the needy.
JOB 34:28 NIV

He shall call upon Me, and I will answer him; I will be with him in
trouble; I will deliver him and honor him.
PSALM 91:15 NKJV

Because he bends down to listen,
I will pray as long as I have breath!
PSALM 116:2 NLT

Is any among you afflicted? let him pray. Is any merry? let him sing psalms. Is any sick among you? let him call for the elders of the church; and let them pray over him, anointing him with oil in the name of the Lord: And the prayer of faith shall save the sick, and the Lord shall raise him up; and if he have committed sins, they shall be forgiven him.

JAMES 5:13–15 KJV

Be anxious for nothing, but in everything by prayer and supplication with thanksgiving let your requests be made known to God. And the peace of God, which surpasses all comprehension, will guard your hearts and your minds in Christ Jesus.

PHILIPPIANS 4:6–7 NASB

Prayer is an indispensable part of our relationship with Jesus Christ.

LAUREL OKE LOGAN

Pride

*H*ave you noticed that boasting has become an admirable attribute? (To clarify: Confidence in one's abilities or talents is different from bragging about them.) With much bravado, women from the boardroom to the catwalk herald their gifts and talents with more intensity than an on-the-scene journalist broadcasting breaking news.

Pride is not only admissible in the world, it's expected. To God, however, pride is sin. A proud and haughty spirit is unattractive and unacceptable to the King of kings. Besides, any king's daughter would rather brag about her heavenly Father's attributes than about her own.

Do not be wise in your own eyes; fear the LORD and shun evil.
PROVERBS 3:7 NIV

And He sat down, called the twelve, and said to them,
"If anyone desires to be first, he shall be last of all
and servant of all."
MARK 9:35 NKJV

But it is wrong to say God doesn't listen,
to say the Almighty isn't concerned.
JOB 35:13 NLT

A high look, and a proud heart,
and the plowing of the wicked, is sin.
PROVERBS 21:4 KJV

But as it is, you boast in your arrogance; all such boasting is evil.
JAMES 4:16 NASB

Live in harmony with one another. Do not be proud,
but be willing to associate with people of low position.
Do not be conceited.
ROMANS 12:16 NIV

Talk no more so very proudly; let no arrogance come from your mouth,
for the LORD is the God of knowledge;
and by Him actions are weighed.
1 SAMUEL 2:3 NKJV

All who fear the LORD will hate evil. Therefore, I hate pride
and arrogance, corruption and perverse speech.
PROVERBS 8:13 NLT

As the Scriptures say, "If you want to boast, boast only about the LORD." When people commend themselves, it doesn't count for much. The important thing is for the Lord to commend them.
2 CORINTHIANS 10:17–18 NLT

How can ye believe, which receive honour one of another, and seek not the honour that cometh from God only?
JOHN 5:44 KJV

Pride goes before destruction, and a haughty spirit before stumbling.
PROVERBS 16:18 NASB

For by the grace given me I say to every one of you: Do not think of yourself more highly than you ought, but rather think of yourself with sober judgment, in accordance with the measure of faith God has given you.
ROMANS 12:3 NIV

For if a man think himself to be something, when he is nothing, he deceiveth himself.
GALATIANS 6:3 KJV

Why are we not far more frightened of what pride can do? Pride can cost us— and probably those after us.
BETH MOORE

Protection

As women, we walk with caution to our car or on the street at night. We warn our daughters to guard themselves against possible intruders or attacks. Mothers use child-safety products to protect toddlers from harm, and we teach our children to avoid strangers and to look both ways before crossing the street.

Similarly, God protects us. He provides a refuge in life's storms with the assurance that He is with us in every situation. He takes extra precaution to guide, assist, instruct, and protect us each day. He is our help, our shield, and our best protection.

The LORD of hosts is with us; the God of Jacob is our refuge. Selah.
PSALM 46:7 KJV

In the fear of the LORD there is strong confidence,
and his children will have refuge.
PROVERBS 14:26 NASB

When you pass through the waters, I will be with you; and when you
pass through the rivers, they will not sweep over you.
When you walk through the fire, you will not be burned;
the flames will not set you ablaze.
ISAIAH 43:2 NIV

But the LORD has been my defense,
and my God the rock of my refuge.
PSALM 94:22 NKJV

Be my rock of safety where I can always hide. Give the order to save me,
for you are my rock and my fortress.
PSALM 71:3 NLT

Above all, taking the shield of faith, wherewith ye shall be
able to quench all the fiery darts of the wicked.
EPHESIANS 6:16 KJV

For it is You who blesses the righteous man, O LORD,
You surround him with favor as with a shield.
PSALM 5:12 NASB

The name of the LORD is a strong fortress;
the godly run to him and are safe.
PROVERBS 18:10 NLT

Our soul waiteth for the LORD: he is our help and our shield.
PSALM 33:20 KJV

Every word of God is tested;
He is a shield to those who take refuge in Him.
PROVERBS 30:5 NASB

He will cover you with his feathers, and under his wings you will find
refuge; his faithfulness will be your shield and rampart.
PSALM 91:4 NIV

But whoever listens to me will dwell safely,
and will be secure, without fear of evil.
PROVERBS 1:33 NKJV

He sang: "The LORD is my rock, my fortress, and my savior; my God is
my rock, in whom I find protection. He is my shield, the power
that saves me, and my place of safety. He is my refuge, my savior,
the one who saves me from violence. I called on the LORD, who is
worthy of praise, and he saved me from my enemies."
2 SAMUEL 22:2–4 NLT

The LORD is my rock, my fortress and my deliverer;
my God is my rock, in whom I take refuge.
He is my shield and the horn of my salvation, my stronghold.
PSALM 18:2 NIV

For You are my rock and my fortress; therefore, for Your name's sake,
lead me and guide me.
PSALM 31:3 NKJV

The LORD is good, a strong hold in the day of trouble;
and he knoweth them that trust in him.

NAHUM 1:7 KJV

Cast your burden upon the LORD and He will sustain you;
He will never allow the righteous to be shaken.

PSALM 55:22 NASB

God is our refuge and strength, always ready to help in
times of trouble. So we will not fear when earthquakes
come and the mountains crumble into the sea.
Let the oceans roar and foam.
Let the mountains tremble as the waters surge!

PSALM 46:1–3 NLT

The eternal God is thy refuge, and underneath are the everlasting arms.

DEUTERONOMY 33:27 KJV

The LORD also will be a stronghold for the oppressed,
a stronghold in times of trouble.

PSALM 9:9 NASB

God is our refuge and strength, an ever-present help in trouble.

PSALM 46:1 NIV

God will never lead you
where His strength
cannot keep you.

BARBARA JOHNSON

Purity

Christians take heart. Purity is gaining popularity. Teenagers across the country are vowing abstinence by wearing "purity rings." The silver band symbolizes a teen's vow to celibacy until marriage——it is an expression of his or her love and commitment to God and the promise to live a pure life.

Whether we are fourteen or fifty, the pledge to purity can begin anytime and carry throughout our lifetime. God calls every believer to a life of holiness without fornication, adultery, or impurity. A pure life is a fully consecrated one, with or without a symbolic ring.

Drink water from your own cistern, and running water from your own well.
PROVERBS 5:15 NKJV

So put to death the sinful, earthly things lurking within you.
Have nothing to do with sexual immorality, impurity, lust,
and evil desires. Don't be greedy, for a greedy person is an
idolater, worshiping the things of this world. Because of these
sins, the anger of God is coming.
COLOSSIANS 3:5–6 NLT

But fornication, and all uncleanness, or covetousness, let it not be once
named among you, as becometh saints.
EPHESIANS 5:3 KJV

You shall not commit adultery.
EXODUS 20:14 NASB

*A person of purity
stands before his peers and superiors
and courageously maintains
his faith in God.*

CINDY TRENT

Repentance

What is repentance? To regret you bought those expensive shoes? To wish you hadn't opened your mouth, or to kick yourself for not speaking up?

To *repent* means to change one's mind, yes. But it also means to turn *away* from sin and turn *toward* God. The Lord cannot forgive us of our sins until we repent of them and turn to Him for salvation.

Did you know that there is a good kind of sorrow? It's the sorrow that leads us to repentance (2 Corinthians 7:10). As we repent, God forgives and our new life begins.

For the sorrow that is according to the will of God produces a repentance without regret, leading to salvation, but the sorrow of the world produces death.
2 CORINTHIANS 7:10 NASB

The Lord is not slack concerning His promise, as some count slackness, but is longsuffering toward us, not willing that any should perish but that all should come to repentance.
2 PETER 3:9 NKJV

God overlooked people's ignorance about these things in earlier times, but now he commands everyone everywhere to repent of their sins and turn to him.
ACTS 17:30 NLT

I will have mercy, and not sacrifice: for I am not come to call the righteous, but sinners to repentance.
MATTHEW 9:13 KJV

In the same way, I tell you, there is joy in the presence of the angels of God over one sinner who repents.
LUKE 15:10 NASB

Remember, therefore, what you have received and heard; obey it, and repent. But if you do not wake up, I will come like a thief, and you will not know at what time I will come to you.
REVELATION 3:3 NIV

Or do you despise the riches of His goodness, forbearance, and longsuffering, not knowing that the goodness of God leads you to repentance?
ROMANS 2:4 NKJV

He will sing to men and say, "I have sinned and perverted what is right, and it is not proper for me. He has redeemed my soul from going to the pit, and my life shall see the light."
JOB 33:27–28 NASB

Rend your heart and not your garments. Return to the LORD your God, for he is gracious and compassionate, slow to anger and abounding in love, and he relents from sending calamity.
JOEL 2:13 NIV

Now repent of your sins and turn to God, so that your sins may be wiped away.
ACTS 3:19 NLT

The LORD is nigh unto them that are of a broken heart; and saveth such as be of a contrite spirit.
PSALM 34:18 KJV

Therefore repent of this wickedness of yours, and pray the Lord that, if possible, the intention of your heart may be forgiven you.
ACTS 8:22 NASB

Come near to God and he will come near to you. Wash your hands, you sinners, and purify your hearts, you double-minded.
JAMES 4:8 NIV

We long for revival,
but revival begins with
repentance.
NATALIE GRANT

Rest

Most women are doers, proficient in multitasking. We cook dinner as we do laundry and assist our kids with homework. We schedule appointments via cell phone while we grocery shop. We answer e-mails while paying bills. And the moment we stop, our minds spin as we relive the day.

Although rest is essential to our spiritual, physical, and emotional health, it often gets lost like a stray sock in the dryer. God wants His people to rest, and this section of scriptures emphasizes the benefits of and need for a break.

So take a breather. Rest.

I will both lay me down in peace, and sleep:
for thou, LORD, only makest me dwell in safety.
PSALM 4:8 KJV

For He has said somewhere concerning the seventh day:
"And God rested on the seventh day from all His works". . .
So there remains a Sabbath rest for the people of God.
HEBREWS 4:4, 9 NASB

And you would be secure, because there is hope;
yes, you would dig around you, and take your rest in safety.
JOB 11:18 NKJV

Those who live in the shelter of the Most High will find rest in
the shadow of the Almighty.
PSALM 91:1 NLT

Rest in the LORD, and wait patiently for him: fret not thyself because
of him who prospereth in his way, because of the man who
bringeth wicked devices to pass.
PSALM 37:7 KJV

*Again and again, I've found Him faithful
to respond, and the closer I move to Him,
the safer I feel and the better I rest.*
PATSY CLAIRMONT

Righteousness

What is righteousness? What can we do to attain it? Is right living the ticket? Or is there something more we should know or do?

The definition of *righteousness* includes the following: "A quality or character of uprightness; an attribute of God and whatever or whoever conforms to the revealed will of God."

Contrary to what some believe, God's righteousness is only attainable through faith in Christ, not through obedience to a prescribed set of laws or good deeds (Ephesians 2:8–9).

Do you desire righteousness? Accept Christ and follow His Word.

Do you not know that the unrighteous will not inherit the kingdom of God?
Do not be deceived. Neither fornicators, nor idolaters,
nor adulterers, nor homosexuals, nor sodomites.
1 Corinthians 6:9 nkjv

> Seek the Kingdom of God above all else,
> and live righteously, and he will give you
> everything you need.
> Matthew 6:33 nlt

Lord, who shall abide in thy tabernacle? who shall dwell in thy holy
hill? He that walketh uprightly, and worketh righteousness,
and speaketh the truth in his heart.
Psalm 15:1–2 kjv

> He does not withdraw His eyes from the righteous;
> but with kings on the throne He has seated them forever,
> and they are exalted.
> Job 36:7 nasb

All your words are true; all your righteous laws are eternal.
Psalm 119:160 niv

> Then the righteous will shine forth as the sun in the kingdom
> of their Father. He who has ears to hear, let him hear!
> Matthew 13:43 nkjv

Whereby are given unto us exceeding great and precious promises:
that by these ye might be partakers of the divine nature,
having escaped the corruption that is in the world through lust.
2 Peter 1:4 kjv

The Lord hears his people when they call to him for help.
He rescues them from all their troubles.
PSALM 34:17 NLT

But if you truly obey his voice and do all that I say, then I will be an
enemy to your enemies and an adversary to your adversaries.
EXODUS 23:22 NASB

If we confess our sins, he is faithful and just and will forgive
us our sins and purify us from all unrighteousness.
1 JOHN 1:9 NIV

You who love the LORD, hate evil! He preserves the souls of His saints;
He delivers them out of the hand of the wicked. Light is sown
for the righteous, and gladness for the upright in heart.
PSALM 97:10–11 NKJV

If you fully obey the Lord your God and carefully keep all his
commands that I am giving you today, the Lord your God
will set you high above all the nations of the world.
DEUTERONOMY 28:1 NLT

The eyes of the LORD are upon the righteous,
and his ears are open unto their cry.
PSALM 34:15 KJV

The Lord will not allow the righteous to hunger,
but He will reject the craving of the wicked.
PROVERBS 10:3 NASB

Whoever pursues righteousness and unfailing love will find life,
righteousness, and honor.
PROVERBS 21:21 NLT

But know that the LORD hath set apart him that is godly for himself: the LORD will hear when I call unto him.

PSALM 4:3 KJV

Then He will answer them, "Truly I say to you, to the extent that you did not do it to one of the least of these, you did not do it to Me. These will go away into eternal punishment, but the righteous into eternal life."

MATTHEW 25:45–46 NASB

Let the righteous rejoice in the LORD and take refuge in him; let all the upright in heart praise him!

PSALM 64:10 NIV

For He made Him who knew no sin to be sin for us, that we might become the righteousness of God in Him.

2 CORINTHIANS 5:21 NKJV

We do not have to be qualified to be holy.

MADELEINE L'ENGLE

Salvation

In the world, work is a prerequisite to achievement. In God's Word, works are meaningless without faith in Christ. Salvation is God's free gift to anyone who confesses her sins and asks Jesus into her heart and life. Why? Because Jesus paid the price for our sins when He died on the cross—and by accepting Him, we are given salvation and eternal life.

Have you asked Jesus into your heart? If not, He stands at your door and knocks. All you need do is invite Him in. Go ahead. He's been waiting awhile.

This means that anyone who belongs to Christ has become a new person.
The old life is gone; a new life has begun!
2 Corinthians 5:17 nlt

My little children, these things write I unto you, that ye sin not.
And if any man sin, we have an advocate with the Father,
Jesus Christ the righteous: And he is the propitiation
for our sins: and not for ours only, but also for the sins
of the whole world.
1 John 2:1–2 kjv

This is good and acceptable in the sight of God our Savior, who desires all
men to be saved and to come to the knowledge of the truth.
1 Timothy 2:3–4 nasb

Yet to all who received him, to those who believed in his
name, he gave the right to become children of God—
children born not of natural descent, nor of human decision
or a husband's will, but born of God.
John 1:12–13 niv

He who believes in the Son has everlasting life; and he who does not believe
the Son shall not see life, but the wrath of God abides on him.
John 3:36 nkjv

There is salvation in no one else! God has given no other
name under heaven by which we must be saved.
Acts 4:12 nlt

But after that the kindness and love of God our Saviour toward man appeared, not by works of righteousness which we have done, but according to his mercy he saved us, by the washing of regeneration, and renewing of the Holy Ghost; which he shed on us abundantly through Jesus Christ our Saviour.
TITUS 3:4–6 KJV

Just as I also please all men in all things, not seeking my own profit but the profit of the many, so that they may be saved.
1 CORINTHIANS 10:33 NASB

In reply Jesus declared, "I tell you the truth, no one can see the kingdom of God unless he is born again." "How can a man be born when he is old?" Nicodemus asked. "Surely he cannot enter a second time into his mother's womb to be born!" Jesus answered, "I tell you the truth, no one can enter the kingdom of God unless he is born of water and the Spirit. Flesh gives birth to flesh, but the Spirit gives birth to spirit. You should not be surprised at my saying, 'You must be born again.'"
JOHN 3:3–7 NIV

Christ has made all things right.
I had nothing to do but accept it as
a free gift from Him.
HANNAH WHITALL SMITH

Scripture

Is the Bible just an ancient history book? What significance do the scriptures have in modern society?

As the following verses indicate, the scriptures are the life-giving, soul-sustaining, power-packed, anointed words of God! They provide us with the spiritual nutrients necessary for daily living.

God's Word reveals God's will and character to us, bringing salvation, healing, deliverance, hope, peace, wisdom, guidance, and restoration to those who read its pages.

Just an ancient history book inapplicable to today's lifestyle and issues? Read on.

Let the word of Christ dwell in you richly in all wisdom, teaching and admonishing one another in psalms and hymns and spiritual songs, singing with grace in your hearts to the Lord.
COLOSSIANS 3:16 NKJV

I have hidden your word in my heart,
that I might not sin against you.
PSALM 119:11 NLT

And that from a child thou hast known the holy scriptures, which are able to make thee wise unto salvation through faith which is in Christ Jesus.
2 TIMOTHY 3:15 KJV

Your word is a lamp to my feet and a light to my path.
PSALM 119:105 NASB

Fix these words of mine in your hearts and minds; tie them as symbols on your hands and bind them on your foreheads. Teach them to your children, talking about them when you sit at home and when you walk along the road, when you lie down and when you get up.
DEUTERONOMY 11:18–19 NIV

For the word of God is living and powerful, and sharper than any two-edged sword, piercing even to the division of soul and spirit, and of joints and marrow, and is a discerner of the thoughts and intents of the heart.
HEBREWS 4:12 NKJV

God, after He spoke long ago to the fathers in the prophets in many portions and in many ways, in these last days has spoken to us in His Son, whom He appointed heir of all things, through whom also He made the world.
HEBREWS 1:1–2 NASB

This Book of the Law shall not depart from your mouth, but you shall meditate in it day and night, that you may observe to do according to all that is written in it. For then you will make your way prosperous, and then you will have good success.

JOSHUA 1:8 NKJV

Searching what, or what manner of time, the Spirit of Christ who was in them was indicating when He testified beforehand the sufferings of Christ and the glories that would follow. To them it was revealed that, not to themselves, but to us they were ministering the things which now have been reported to you through those who have preached the gospel to you by the Holy Spirit sent from heaven—things which angels desire to look into.
1 PETER 1:11–12 NKJV

How much of a calm and gentle spirit you achieve, then, will depend on how regularly and consistently, persistently and obediently you partake of the Word of God, your spiritual food.

SHIRLEY RICE

Seeking God

I once lost my then-small son in an interactive playroom at Disney World. Panic set in as I scoured every area. About to notify security, I raced to the escalator where Jeff stood sobbing. "Where were you?" he whimpered, as if I was the one who was lost.

Similarly, God isn't lost—we are. Our search for Him begins when we realize that. Most of us seek God when we're afraid, discouraged, sick, or sad. But God desires for us to seek Him because we yearn to know Him. These passages reveal how God blesses and rewards those who diligently seek Him.

But seek ye first the kingdom of God, and his righteousness;
and all these things shall be added unto you.
MATTHEW 6:33 KJV

Sow with a view to righteousness, reap in accordance with
kindness; break up your fallow ground, for it is time to seek
the LORD until He comes to rain righteousness on you.
HOSEA 10:12 NASB

Look to the LORD and his strength; seek his face always.
1 CHRONICLES 16:11 NIV

Glory in His holy name; let the hearts of those rejoice
who seek the LORD!
1 CHRONICLES 16:10 NKJV

If you look for me wholeheartedly, you will find me.
JEREMIAH 29:13 NLT

One thing have I desired of the LORD, that will I seek after; that
I may dwell in the house of the LORD all the days of my life, to
behold the beauty of the LORD, and to enquire in his temple.
PSALM 27:4 KJV

At night my soul longs for You, indeed, my spirit within me seeks You
diligently; for when the earth experiences Your judgments the
inhabitants of the world learn righteousness.
ISAIAH 26:9 NASB

But from there you will search again for the LORD your God.
And if you search for him with all your heart and soul,
you will find him.
DEUTERONOMY 4:29 NLT

Seek the LORD, and ye shall live.
AMOS 5:6 KJV

> Therefore if you have been raised up with Christ,
> keep seeking the things above, where Christ is,
> seated at the right hand of God.
> COLOSSIANS 3:1 NASB

Glory in his holy name;
let the hearts of those who seek the LORD rejoice.
1 CHRONICLES 16:10 NIV

> The young lions lack and suffer hunger;
> but those who seek the LORD shall not lack any good thing.
> PSALM 34:10 NKJV

Then if my people who are called by my name will humble themselves and pray and
seek my face and turn from their wicked ways, I will hear from heaven and
will forgive their sins and restore their land.
2 CHRONICLES 7:14 NLT

*For it is impossible to be in the
presence of Jesus
and not be changed.*
JOANNA WEAVER

Self-Control

Pastries line the table. "Have one," the hostess says. "Thanks, but I'm dieting," you respond. "One won't hurt," she prods, handing you a chocolate tart. Soon one tart turns into three with a side dish of strawberry cheesecake. "I'll resume my diet tomorrow," you reason, self-control scrambling away faster than rats from a burning building.

When we act, say, go, or do what we shouldn't, we lose control—and end up regretting it. The Bible teaches that self-control and moderation is achievable. Our desires may tempt us, but they don't have to control us. Even while we're dieting!

Then Pilate said to Him, "Do You not hear how many things they testify against You?" And He did not answer him with regard to even a single charge, so the governor was quite amazed.
MATTHEW 27:13–14 NASB

But even the archangel Michael, when he was disputing with the devil about the body of Moses, did not dare to bring a slanderous accusation against him, but said, "The Lord rebuke you!"
JUDE 9 NIV

For to this you were called, because Christ also suffered for us, leaving us an example, that you should follow His steps: "Who committed no sin, nor was deceit found in His mouth"; who, when He was reviled, did not revile in return; when He suffered, He did not threaten, but committed Himself to Him who judges righteously.
1 PETER 2:21–23 NKJV

Do you like honey? Don't eat too much, or it will make you sick!
PROVERBS 25:16 NLT

Charity suffereth long, and is kind; charity envieth not; charity vaunteth not itself, is not puffed up, doth not behave itself unseemly, seeketh not her own, is not easily provoked, thinketh no evil.
1 CORINTHIANS 13:4–5 KJV

Let your gentle spirit be known to all men. The Lord is near.
PHILIPPIANS 4:5 NASB

Because we belong to the day, we must live decent lives for all to see. Don't participate in the darkness of wild parties and drunkenness, or in sexual promiscuity and immoral living, or in quarreling and jealousy. Instead, clothe yourself with the presence of the Lord Jesus Christ. And don't let yourself think about ways to indulge your evil desires.
ROMANS 13:13–14 NLT

And beside this, giving all diligence, add to your faith virtue; and to virtue knowledge; And to knowledge temperance; and to temperance patience; and to patience godliness.
2 PETER 1:5–6 KJV

Older men are to be temperate, dignified, sensible, sound in faith, in love, in perseverance.
TITUS 2:2 NASB

Everyone who competes in the games goes into strict training. They do it to get a crown that will not last; but we do it to get a crown that will last forever.
1 CORINTHIANS 9:25 NIV

Let him sit alone and keep silent, because God has laid it on him; let him put his mouth in the dust—there may yet be hope.
LAMENTATIONS 3:28–29 NKJV

And we are instructed to turn from godless living and sinful pleasures. We should live in this evil world with wisdom, righteousness, and devotion to God.
TITUS 2:12 NLT

Do you not know that the wicked will not inherit the kingdom of God? Do not be deceived: Neither the sexually immoral nor idolaters nor adulterers nor male prostitutes nor homosexual offenders nor thieves nor the greedy nor drunkards nor slanderers nor swindlers will inherit the kingdom of God. And that is what some of you were. But you were washed, you were sanctified, you were justified in the name of the Lord Jesus Christ and by the Spirit of our God.
1 CORINTHIANS 6:9–11 NIV

For if you live according to the flesh you will die;
but if by the Spirit you put to death the deeds of the body,
you will live.
ROMANS 8:13 NKJV

Rules for proper behavior keep us from getting hurt. We risk our own life and the lives of others when we give in to our desires, whatever they might be.

LINDA BARTLETT

Sin

$\mathcal{S}$ome think that *sin* is too harsh a word. So they use euphemisms for sin such as *mistake, blunder, fault, offense,* or *violation,* which sound much better. We might try to whitewash it, but sin is just that—sin.

The scriptures define *sin* as knowing to do good but not doing it. No one is blameless. We have all sinned and are in need of repentance and forgiveness.

Jesus came to fix the sin problem. Just ask Him. He's not afraid of the word *sin*—He conquered it!

But if we walk in the Light as He Himself is in the Light, we have fellowship with one another, and the blood of Jesus His Son cleanses us from all sin.
1 JOHN 1:7 NASB

"Come now, let us reason together," says the LORD. "Though your sins are like scarlet, they shall be as white as snow; though they are red as crimson, they shall be like wool."
ISAIAH 1:18 NIV

For this is My blood of the new covenant, which is shed for many for the remission of sins.
MATTHEW 26:28 NKJV

But he was pierced for our rebellion, crushed for our sins. He was beaten so we could be whole. He was whipped so we could be healed. All of us, like sheep, have strayed away. We have left God's paths to follow our own. Yet the LORD laid on him the sins of us all.
ISAIAH 53:5–6 NLT

My little children, these things write I unto you, that ye sin not. And if any man sin, we have an advocate with the Father, Jesus Christ the righteous: And he is the propitiation for our sins: and not for ours only, but also for the sins of the whole world.
1 JOHN 2:1–2 KJV

Of Him all the prophets bear witness that through His name everyone who believes in Him receives forgiveness of sins.
ACTS 10:43 NASB

Here is a trustworthy saying that deserves full acceptance: Christ Jesus came into the world to save sinners—of whom I am the worst.
1 TIMOTHY 1:15 NIV

Who Himself bore our sins in His own body on the tree, that we, having died to sins, might live for righteousness— by whose stripes you were healed.
1 PETER 2:24 NKJV

He has removed our sins as far from us as the east is from the west.
PSALM 103:12 NLT

Knowing this, that our old man is crucified with him, that the body of sin might be destroyed, that henceforth we should not serve sin. For he that is dead is freed from sin.
ROMANS 6:6–7 KJV

Who gave Himself for our sins so that He might rescue us from this present evil age, according to the will of our God and Father.
GALATIANS 1:4 NASB

It is the very nature of sin to prevent man from meditating on spiritual things.
MARY MARTHA SHERWOOD

Sincerity

$\mathcal{S}$incerity is as welcoming as nestling in a cozy chair in front of a fire on a brisk, cold day.

The motives behind what we say or do are at the core of a sincere heart. Are our motives pure and genuine? Or do we possess a selfish, hidden agenda? Someone who demonstrates sincerity of heart and pure motives is a person whom we can trust.

Similarly, God expects us to approach Him in a straightforward manner with unadulterated sincerity. Hypocrisy has no place in our relationship with Him. God knows our heart and He seeks one seeped in sincerity.

Blessed is the man whose sin the LORD does not count against him and in whose spirit is no deceit.
PSALM 32:2 NIV

And in their mouth was found no deceit,
for they are without fault before the throne of God.
REVELATION 14:5 NKJV

So think clearly and exercise self-control. Look forward to the gracious salvation that will come to you when Jesus Christ is revealed to the world.
1 PETER 1:13 NLT

But let us, who are of the day, be sober, putting on the breastplate of faith and love; and for an helmet, the hope of salvation.
1 THESSALONIANS 5:8 KJV

Like newborn babies, long for the pure milk of the word, so that by it you may grow in respect to salvation.
1 PETER 2:2 NASB

Grace to all who love our Lord Jesus Christ
with an undying love.
EPHESIANS 6:24 NIV

For we are not, as so many, peddling the word of God; but as of sincerity, but as from God, we speak in the sight of God in Christ.
2 CORINTHIANS 2:17 NKJV

So fear the Lord and serve him wholeheartedly.
Put away forever the idols your ancestors worshiped when
they lived beyond the Euphrates River and in Egypt.
Serve the Lord alone.
JOSHUA 24:14 NLT

Now that you have purified yourselves by obeying the truth so that you have
sincere love for your brothers, love one another deeply, from the heart.
1 PETER 1:22 NIV

What will you do in the appointed day,
and in the day of the feast of the Lord?
HOSEA 9:5 NKJV

We can say with confidence and a clear conscience that we have lived with a God-
given holiness and sincerity in all our dealings. We have depended on God's
grace, not on our own human wisdom. That is how we have
conducted ourselves before the world, and especially toward you.
2 CORINTHIANS 1:12 NLT

For our exhortation was not of deceit, nor of uncleanness,
nor in guile: But as we were allowed of God to be put in
trust with the gospel, even so we speak; not as pleasing
men, but God, which trieth our hearts. For neither at any
time used we flattering words, as ye know,
nor a cloke of covetousness; God is witness.
1 THESSALONIANS 2:3–5 KJV

Therefore let us celebrate the feast, not with old leaven, nor with the
leaven of malice and wickedness, but with the unleavened bread
of sincerity and truth.
1 CORINTHIANS 5:8 NASB

Therefore, rid yourselves of all malice and all deceit,
hypocrisy, envy, and slander of every kind.
1 PETER 2:1 NIV

For I say, through the grace given to me, to everyone who is among you,
not to think of himself more highly than he ought to think, but
to think soberly, as God has dealt to each one a measure of faith.
ROMANS 12:3 NKJV

For I want you to understand what really matters,
so that you may live pure and blameless lives
until the day of Christ's return.
PHILIPPIANS 1:10 NLT

I speak not by commandment, but by occasion of the forwardness of
others, and to prove the sincerity of your love.
2 CORINTHIANS 8:8 KJV

Speaking beautifully is
little to the purpose
unless one lives beautifully.

ELIZABETH PRENTISS

Sobriety

*S*obriety includes several areas of behavior. Some scriptures refer to *soberness* as soundness of mind or exhibiting self-control. In other verses, *sobriety* addresses the negative influence of alcohol and intoxicants.

Either way, these passages direct us to be filled with God's Spirit rather than substances or attitudes that will control and destroy our lives. The damages intoxicants inflict are far-reaching, leading us into bondage. The scriptures warn us to flee from the things that have the potential to harm ourselves and others. So be sober, filled to overflowing with the Holy Spirit.

For he will be great in the sight of the Lord. He is never to take wine or other fermented drink, and he will be filled with the Holy Spirit even from birth.
LUKE 1:15 NIV

Wine produces mockers; alcohol leads to brawls. Those led astray by drink cannot be wise.
PROVERBS 20:1 NLT

Woe unto them that rise up early in the morning, that they may follow strong drink; that continue until night, till wine inflame them!
ISAIAH 5:11 KJV

They have also cast lots for My people, traded a boy for a harlot and sold a girl for wine that they may drink.
JOEL 3:3 NASB

Who has woe? Who has sorrow? Who has strife? Who has complaints? Who has needless bruises? Who has bloodshot eyes? Those who linger over wine, who go to sample bowls of mixed wine. Do not gaze at wine when it is red, when it sparkles in the cup, when it goes down smoothly! In the end it bites like a snake and poisons like a viper.
PROVERBS 23:29–32 NIV

Now therefore, please be careful not to drink wine or similar drink, and not to eat anything unclean.
JUDGES 13:4 NKJV

What sorrow awaits you who make your neighbors drunk! You force your cup on them so you can gloat over their shameful nakedness.
HABAKKUK 2:15 NLT

And take heed to yourselves, lest at any time your hearts be overcharged with surfeiting, and drunkenness, and cares of this life, and so that day come upon you unawares.

LUKE 21:34 KJV

Like tangled thorns, and like those who are drunken with their drink, they are consumed as stubble completely withered.

NAHUM 1:10 NASB

For drunkards and gluttons become poor, and drowsiness clothes them in rags.

PROVERBS 23:21 NIV

"Abstain," says God. He doesn't say, "Be careful" or "Pray about it." He says, "Abstain! Run from it! Don't touch it! Have nothing to do with it!" Stay pure and blameless. If you don't, God will suffer most of all.

ANNE ORTLUND

Strength

Why do we wait until our strength is depleted before we seek God?

Women carry the weight of the world on their shoulders. We worry about our families as we manage our homes and assist our friends, churches, and communities. We maintain busy schedules as we transport kids to soccer practice and school functions. We cook, clean, work, and care for aging parents. No wonder we run out of steam!

Yet God wants us to rely upon His strength, not ours—to exchange our weakness for His power. What are you waiting for? Seek God's strength.

For the eyes of the LORD run to and fro throughout the whole earth, to show Himself strong on behalf of those whose heart is loyal to Him. In this you have done foolishly; therefore from now on you shall have wars.
2 CHRONICLES 16:9 NKJV

Wealth and honor come from you alone, for you rule over everything. Power and might are in your hand, and at your discretion people are made great and given strength.
1 CHRONICLES 29:12 NLT

Finally, my brethren, be strong in the Lord, and in the power of his might.
EPHESIANS 6:10 KJV

In purity, in knowledge, in patience, in kindness, in the Holy Spirit, in genuine love, in the word of truth, in the power of God; by the weapons of righteousness for the right hand and the left.
2 CORINTHIANS 6:6–7 NASB

He gives strength to the weary and increases the power of the weak.
ISAIAH 40:29 NIV

Wait on the LORD; be of good courage, and He shall strengthen your heart; wait, I say, on the LORD!
PSALM 27:14 NKJV

The LORD gives his people strength. The LORD blesses them with peace.
PSALM 29:11 NLT

The righteous keep moving forward, and those with clean hands become stronger and stronger.
JOB 17:9 NLT

That ye might walk worthy of the Lord unto all pleasing, being fruitful in every good work, and increasing in the knowledge of God; strengthened with all might, according to his glorious power, unto all patience and longsuffering with joyfulness.
COLOSSIANS 1:10–11 KJV

> O God, You are awesome from Your sanctuary. The God of Israel Himself gives strength and power to the people. Blessed be God!
> PSALM 68:35 NASB

But he said to me, "My grace is sufficient for you, for my power is made perfect in weakness." Therefore I will boast all the more gladly about my weaknesses, so that Christ's power may rest on me.
2 CORINTHIANS 12:9 NIV

We must continue to
ask God for wisdom and insight and for
the strength to persevere.
He will cause us to rise up
and fly like eagles,
walking and not fainting.

NORMA SMALLEY

Temptation

Jesus fasted and prayed in the wilderness for forty days and the devil tempted Him, albeit unsuccessfully.

Our Savior faced temptation, and so do we. Although it presents itself in different forms, temptation is what Satan uses to defeat, discourage, and pollute the believer's mind and heart. He will use every nasty trick and deceptive device to get us to sin.

But don't worry. Martin Luther once said that we can't stop a bird from flying over our heads, but we can prevent it from building a nest there. Temptation will come—but it need not set up housekeeping.

Let no man say when he is tempted, I am tempted of God: for God cannot be tempted with evil, neither tempteth he any man.
JAMES 1:13 KJV

And do not lead us into temptation, but deliver us from evil.
[For Yours is the kingdom and the power and the glory forever. Amen.]
MATTHEW 6:13 NASB

If this is so, then the Lord knows how to rescue godly men from trials and to hold the unrighteous for the day of judgment, while continuing their punishment.
2 PETER 2:9 NIV

Watch and pray, lest you enter into temptation. The spirit indeed is willing, but the flesh is weak.
MATTHEW 26:41 NKJV

There hath no temptation taken you but such as is common to man: but God is faithful, who will not suffer you to be tempted above that ye are able; but will with the temptation also make a way to escape, that ye may be able to bear it.
1 CORINTHIANS 10:13 KJV

*Temptations come,
as a general rule,
when they are sought.*
MARGARET OLIPHANT

Truth

Your child gets in trouble at school. You question her, insisting on the whole truth. The doctor has bad news. You want the truth, despite your fear and hesitation.

In situations like these, truth becomes all-important. Yet truth is even more essential in our walk with God.

In the Bible, the idea of *truth* carries four interpretations: 1) actual, true to fact; 2) real, ideal, genuine; 3) dealing faithfully or truly with others; and 4) truth in all its fullness and scope, as embodied in Jesus, showing sincerity and integrity of character.

To know Jesus is to know the truth.

Buy the truth, and do not sell it, also wisdom and
instruction and understanding.
PROVERBS 23:23 NKJV

> For the LORD is good. His unfailing love continues forever,
> and his faithfulness continues to each generation.
> PSALM 100:5 NLT

Jesus saith unto him, I am the way, the truth, and the life:
no man cometh unto the Father, but by me.
JOHN 14:6 KJV

> The Rock! His work is perfect, for all His ways are just;
> a God of faithfulness and without injustice,
> righteous and upright is He.
> DEUTERONOMY 32:4 NASB

Finally, brothers, whatever is true, whatever is noble, whatever
is right, whatever is pure, whatever is lovely, whatever is
admirable—if anything is excellent or praiseworthy—
think about such things.
PHILIPPIANS 4:8 NIV

> And you shall know the truth,
> and the truth shall make you free.
> JOHN 8:32 NKJV

All who invoke a blessing or take an oath will do so by the God of truth.
For I will put aside my anger and forget the evil of earlier days.
ISAIAH 65:16 NLT

For the word of the LORD is right;
and all his works are done in truth.
PSALM 33:4 KJV

For their sakes I sanctify Myself, that they themselves also may be
sanctified in truth.
JOHN 17:19 NASB

These are the things you are to do: Speak the truth to each
other, and render true and sound judgment in your courts.
ZECHARIAH 8:16 NIV

For the law was given through Moses, but grace and truth came
through Jesus Christ.
JOHN 1:17 NKJV

If we are Christians,
we have committed ourselves to
the Lord Jesus Christ
who said, "I am the Truth."
In giving ourselves to Him,
we dedicate ourselves to the truth
not only about Him but about ourselves.

PAMELA HOOVER HEIM

Understanding

Eleanor Roosevelt said, "Understanding is a two-way street." We'd all like to be understood, but do we understand? To gain understanding we must consider another's perspective apart from our own. In essence, we must walk in their shoes.

Knowing God gives us a greater appreciation for and understanding of others. As we view people and life through His eyes, our viewpoint changes. The things we once questioned, we now perceive with greater clarity and purpose.

To understand rather than to be understood is every Christian woman's quest for spiritual maturity. To understand while seldom understood is that quest realized.

Joyful is the person who finds wisdom, the one who gains understanding. For wisdom is more profitable than silver, and her wages are better than gold. Wisdom is more precious than rubies; nothing you desire can compare with her.
PROVERBS 3:13–15 NLT

Then shalt thou understand the fear of the LORD, and find the knowledge of God. For the LORD giveth wisdom: out of his mouth cometh knowledge and understanding.
PROVERBS 2:5–6 KJV

They will not hurt or destroy in all My holy mountain, for the earth will be full of the knowledge of the LORD as the waters cover the sea. Then in that day the nations will resort to the root of Jesse, who will stand as a signal for the peoples; and His resting place will be glorious.
ISAIAH 11:9–10 NASB

For wisdom will enter your heart, and knowledge will be pleasant to your soul. Discretion will protect you, and understanding will guard you. Wisdom will save you from the ways of wicked men, from men whose words are perverse.
PROVERBS 2:10–12 NIV

Therefore if there is any consolation in Christ, if any comfort of love, if any fellowship of the Spirit, if any affection and mercy, fulfill my joy by being like-minded, having the same love, being of one accord, of one mind.
PHILIPPIANS 2:1–2 NKJV

When I was a child, I used to speak like a child,
think like a child, reason like a child; when I became a man,
I did away with childish things.

1 CORINTHIANS 13:11 NASB

Wisdom is found on the lips of the discerning,
but a rod is for the back of him who lacks judgment.
PROVERBS 10:13 NIV

But You, O Lord, are a God full of compassion, and
gracious, longsuffering and abundant in mercy and truth.
PSALM 86:15 NKJV

And this is what he says to all humanity: "The fear of the Lord is true
wisdom; to forsake evil is real understanding."
JOB 28:28 NLT

With the ancient is wisdom; and in length of days
understanding. With him is wisdom and strength,
he hath counsel and understanding.
JOB 12:12–13 KJV

Wisdom rests in the heart of one who has understanding,
but in the hearts of fools it is made known.
PROVERBS 14:33 NASB

"But let him who boasts boast about this:
that he understands and knows me, that I am the LORD,
who exercises kindness, justice and righteousness on earth,
for in these I delight," declares the LORD.
JEREMIAH 9:24 NIV

Foolishness brings joy to those with no sense;
a sensible person stays on the right path.
PROVERBS 15:21 NLT

The mind of the prudent acquires knowledge,
and the ear of the wise seeks knowledge.
PROVERBS 18:15 NASB

For if you possess these qualities in increasing measure, they will keep you
from being ineffective and unproductive in your knowledge of
our Lord Jesus Christ.
2 PETER 1:8 NIV

Make me understand the way of Your precepts;
so shall I meditate on Your wonderful works.
PSALM 119:27 NKJV

Rich people may think they are wise, but a poor person with discernment
can see right through them.
PROVERBS 28:11 NLT

Teach me good judgment and knowledge:
for I have believed thy commandments.
PSALM 119:66 KJV

*Yearn to understand first and to be
understood second.*

BECA LEWIS ALLEN

Wisdom

According to Webster's dictionary, *wisdom* is "the power of judging correctly, following the soundest course of action based on knowledge, experience, understanding and good judgment."

God is wisdom personified. His wisdom far exceeds our most impressive reaches of thought. The scriptures explain that "the foolishness of God is wiser than men; and the weakness of God is stronger than men" (1 Corinthians 1:25 KJV). God alone is the source of true wisdom. Accordingly, we should seek His wisdom and discernment in every decision we make. To do so is just plain wise.

Be wise now therefore, O ye kings:
be instructed, ye judges of the earth.
PSALM 2:10 KJV

Those who obey him will not be punished. Those who are
wise will find a time and a way to do what is right.
ECCLESIASTES 8:5 NLT

Say to wisdom, "You are my sister," and call understanding
your intimate friend.
PROVERBS 7:4 NASB

Therefore do not be foolish,
but understand what the Lord's will is.
EPHESIANS 5:17 NIV

Therefore whoever hears these sayings of Mine, and does them, I will liken
him to a wise man who built his house on the rock: and the rain
descended, the floods came, and the winds blew and beat on that
house; and it did not fall, for it was founded on the rock.
MATTHEW 7:24–25 NKJV

It is foolish to belittle one's neighbor;
a sensible person keeps quiet.
PROVERBS 11:12 NLT

A prudent man foreseeth the evil, and hideth himself:
but the simple pass on, and are punished.
PROVERBS 22:3 KJV

A prudent man conceals knowledge,
but the heart of fools proclaims foolishness.
PROVERBS 12:23 NKJV

Good comes to those who lend money generously and conduct their business fairly.
PSALM 112:5 NLT

> He that handleth a matter wisely shall find good:
> and whoso trusteth in the LORD, happy is he. The wise
> in heart shall be called prudent: and the sweetness
> of the lips increaseth learning.
> PROVERBS 16:20–21 KJV

Whoever is wise, let him understand these things; whoever is discerning, let him know them for the ways of the LORD are right, and the righteous will walk in them, but transgressors will stumble in them.
HOSEA 14:9 NASB

> My son, pay attention to what I say; listen closely to my
> words. Do not let them out of your sight, keep them within
> your heart; for they are life to those who find them and
> health to a man's whole body.
> PROVERBS 4:20–22 NIV

The law of the wise is a fountain of life, to turn one away from the snares of death. Good understanding gains favor, but the way of the unfaithful is hard.
PROVERBS 13:14–15 NKJV

> How much better it is to get wisdom than gold!
> And to get understanding is to be chosen above silver.
> PROVERBS 16:16 NASB

To him belong strength and victory; both deceived and deceiver are his.
He leads counselors away stripped and makes fools of judges.
Job 12:16–17 niv

My son, eat honey because it is good, and the honeycomb
which is sweet to your taste; so shall the knowledge of
wisdom be to your soul; if you have found it, there is a
prospect, and your hope will not be cut off.
Proverbs 24:13–14 nkjv

In that day he will be your sure foundation, providing a rich store of
salvation, wisdom, and knowledge. The fear of the Lord
will be your treasure.
Isaiah 33:6 nlt

I will instruct thee and teach thee in the way which thou
shalt go: I will guide thee with mine eye.
Psalm 32:8 kjv

But if any of you lacks wisdom, let him ask of God, who gives to all
generously and without reproach, and it will be given to him.
James 1:5 nasb

A simple man believes anything,
but a prudent man gives thought to his steps.
Proverbs 14:15 niv

For wisdom is protection just as money is protection,
but the advantage of knowledge is that
wisdom preserves the lives of its possessors.
Ecclesiastes 7:12 nasb

However, we speak wisdom among those who are mature, yet not the wisdom of this age, nor of the rulers of this age, who are coming to nothing. But we speak the wisdom of God in a mystery, the hidden wisdom which God ordained before the ages for our glory, which none of the rulers of this age knew; for had they known, they would not have crucified the Lord of glory.
1 CORINTHIANS 2:6–8 NKJV

Those who are wise will take all this to heart;
they will see in our history the faithful love of the LORD.
PSALM 107:43 NLT

And if any man think that he knoweth any thing,
he knoweth nothing yet as he ought to know.
1 CORINTHIANS 8:2 KJV

*Learning is not attained
by chance, it must be sought for
with ardor and attended to with diligence.*

ABIGAIL ADAMS

Zeal

What comes to mind when you hear the word *zeal*? Slobbering sports fans? Wild-eyed fanatics? For most of us, those images aren't terribly appealing.

But the Bible's picture of zeal is different. It's an image of commitment—of God to His people, and His people back to Him. Scriptural zeal is a beautiful thing, a strong desire to do right by God and His creation.

You can't go wrong being zealous for God. A passion for serving Him—by serving the people around you—doesn't make you a fanatic. It makes you like Jesus!

For zeal for your house consumes me, and the insults of those who insult you fall on me.
PSALM 69:9 NIV

Whatsoever thy hand findeth to do, do it with thy might; for there is no work, nor device, nor knowledge, nor wisdom, in the grave, whither thou goest.
ECCLESIASTES 9:10 KJV

He put on righteousness like a breastplate, and a helmet of salvation on His head; And He put on garments of vengeance for clothing and wrapped Himself with zeal as a mantle.
ISAIAH 59:17 NASB

Even so you, since you are zealous for spiritual gifts, let it be for the edification of the church that you seek to excel.
1 CORINTHIANS 14:12 NKJV

As many as I love, I rebuke and chasten: be zealous therefore, and repent.
REVELATION 3:19 KJV

Zeal will do more than knowledge.
WILLIAM HAZLITT